STRAIGHT OUT OF HELL 2

THE TRUE CHARACTER OF A MAN

CRIMINAL JUSTICE SYSTEM, MASS
INCARCERATION & RESTORATION

VMH™ Publishing
Atlanta, GA

STRAIGHT OUT OF HELL 2

THE TRUE CHARACTER OF A MAN

CRIMINAL JUSTICE SYSTEM, MASS INCARCERATION & RESTORATION

GARRY L. JONES

Copyright © 2021 by Garry L. Jones
(2nd Edition)

All rights reserved. In accordance with the U.S. Copyright Act of 1976, the scanning, uploading, and electronic sharing of any part of this book without permission of the publisher constitute unlawful piracy and theft of the author's intellectual property. If you would like to use material from the book (other than for review purposes), prior written permission must be obtained by contacting the publisher at info@vmhpublishing.com.

Thank you for your support of the author's rights.

VMH ™ Publishing
3355 Lenox Rd. NE Suite 750
Atlanta, GA 30326
www.vmhpublishing.com

The publisher is not responsible for websites, or social media pages (or their content) related to this publication, that are not owned by the publisher. Quantity sales. Special discounts are available on quantity purchases by corporations, associations, and others. For details, contact the publisher via email at: info@vmhpublishing.com

Hardback ISBN: 978-0-9984553-3-4

Paperback ISBN: 978-0-9984553-5-8

10 9 8 7 6 5 4 3 2 1

Author's Note:

The names and characters have been changed to protect the privacy of such individual's. The events documented in this publication are according to the author's memory. *The publisher is not responsible for websites, or social media pages (or their content) that are not owned by the publisher.*

Published in United States of America

10 9 8 7 6 5 4 3 2 1

It was a travesty to work at six different prisons in three different states and see the same things occur in each of these prisons. Though there has been extensive media coverage about prisons, and though many politicians have made emotional decisions/laws concerning some of the contents in this book, the 'inside truth' has yet to be told. The things I have witnessed and been subjected to while working inside different prison walls, places me in a position to tell the 'inside truth;' the 'inside truth' about the criminal justice system, that can't be told by others.

In this publication you will encounter the language of truth and reality that may at times seem offensive. My intent is not to offend or make anyone uncomfortable, but to share the facts of my life, without "watering-down" the truth. Names have been changed to protect the privacy of those I speak of.

Garry L. Jones,
Retired Lieutenant Federal Bureau of Prisons

TABLE OF CONTENTS

My Testimony 1

Acknowledgements 3

CHAPTER 1: Lorton 5

CHAPTER 2: My First Day at Work 13

CHAPTER 3: My First Fight as a Rookie 17

CHAPTER 4: Guns on the Inside 23

CHAPTER 5: Losing My Cool 27

CHAPTER 6: Working the Visitation Room 31

CHAPTER 7: My Last Fight at Lorton 37

CHAPTER 8: Leaving Lorton 41

CHAPTER 9: Triangle Correctional Institution 43

CHAPTER 10: The First Day on the Job 47

CHAPTER 11: Wake Correctional Center 57

CHAPTER 12: Officer Jackass 65

CHAPTER 13: Getting Married, The Hell Begins 71

CHAPTER 14: Goldsboro Correctional Center Caseloads 79

CHAPTER 15: Federal Prison Camp Seymour Johnson 87

CHAPTER 16: My First House 95

CHAPTER 17: Special Investigative Supervisor 105

CHAPTER 18: F.C.I. Tallahassee, Tallahassee Florida 109

CHAPTER 19: The Boys in Blue Again 115

CHAPTER 20: The First Working Day at F.C.I. Tallahassee ...121

CHAPTER 21: Riots at F.C.I. Marianna 129

CHAPTER 22: Chaos after the Riot 137

CHAPTER 23: Burned Out 143

CHAPTER 24: The Spark from the Light Gave Him Away ..151

CHAPTER 25: F. Lee Bailey 159

CHAPTER 26: David Anthony Mack # 12866-112 167

CHAPTER 27: Racial Disparities/Federal Parole 171

CHAPTER 28: Working for a New Supervisor and a New Warden 177

CHAPTER 29: The Captain from Hell 181

CHAPTER 30: Food Strike at Tallahassee 189

CHAPTER 31: Fair Sentencing Act of 2010 195

CHAPTER 32: How It All Began 199

CHAPTER 33: A New Presidency Voted In 203

Epilogue 207

References 211

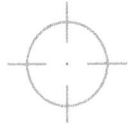

My Testimony

I didn't write this book to demean anyone but I want to share the truth as I saw it yesterday, as I see it today, and tomorrow if God allows me to live another day. This book will take you on a journey to the second part of my life. The first part of my life will be shared at another time, but it was important to allow the second book to be published first only because of the information in it. Now I've come to understand that timing is everything when it comes to God and what his purpose is in your life. This is the season that I believe God wanted this book published.

I would never have known that the country I grew up in and the government I worked for would cause me so much pain as an employee. Neither did I know the country that I grew up in would cause so much unjustifiable oppression towards minorities through unjust laws. As long as my mouth was shut it was OK. When I started seeing the injustice inflicted on people and speaking about it, all hell came upon me.

As you read this book, I ask that you pray for the defenseless and if you have already been praying, I ask that you continue. There is strength in numbers and you are one in that number.

Sincerely Yours,
Garry Lamonte Jones

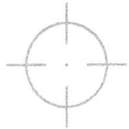

Acknowledgements

I would like to thank my friend and childhood neighbor Mr. Maurice Van Buren Parker for inspiring me to work on my first book thirteen years ago, entitled *Straight Out Of Hell, Wrong Place Wrong Time*. I would like to thank Vikki Marie Hankins, who further inspired me through her time and dedication in publishing my collection of memoirs/books. She made me reach down in my soul and bring the truth out even when I got mad and said I couldn't do this anymore. She continues to say, *'The world needs to read about your experience so other people can learn and grow.'*

My family groomed and shaped me into the man I have become by never discouraging me, and by being positive even when my life and health were at stake. My grandmother, Tessie Simmons Jones, the source of my strength; (Deceased) my mother Vergie Marie Chalmers, my lovely aunts Mavis Colleen Jones, Denderant Jones Burney (Deceased) Mamie Jean Johnson, (Deceased) Mary Lee Mason (Deceased), and the late and great Arnetta Louise Dixon (Deceased). Uncle Earl (Hamm) Jones. (Deceased). My Uncle John Wesley Jones (Jay), my brother

Terry Jones (Pete), sister Lisa Jones, father Milton Dover Jr., and my cousin Annie Mae Grimes Burt.

I would like to thank my children and grandchildren, (Derrick, Daughter in Law Sherrie, (Deceased) LaToya, Malcolm, Dereon, and Jada). Looking at them when they were growing up made me want to fight for justice even harder.

Also friends that helped me fight during our careers with the Federal Bureau of Prisons, Lieutenant Eric Caldwell Jr. (R.I.P.), and Lieutenant Carol Walkerfountaine (Retired BOP Staff).

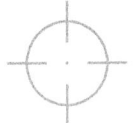

CHAPTER 1

Lorton

I graduated from North Carolina Central University in May 1986. In August 1986, less than one year after I'd gotten shot in a night club, I was working part time at Dobbs Reformatory School, a school for young kids that were too young to go to prison. I was hoping for a full time job because I couldn't find a job with Adult Probation and Parole.

Before I left school, I'd done my internship with Adult Probation and Parole. I didn't realize Adult Probation and Parole positions were based on your political affiliation. A person was more likely to get a job in this field if he/she is a member of the party (Republican or Democratic) that runs the country.

After all of the applications I'd submitted for the Adult Probation and Parole positions, I was granted one interview. I aced the interview, but didn't know anyone on the inside, so I was out of luck. I have an old saying when it comes to jobs, "It's not what you know, but it's 'who' you know and blow."

I'm not trying to discourage anyone from getting their college education, but students need to know this.

Most graduates have big dreams. Some students feel if they have a degree, they will be able to get a job quicker. A lot of times, it does not work that way. Most graduates don't even work in the field in which they received their degree. I'm not being negative, but kids need to know that politics and skin color have a lot to do with whether or not they get a job or a promotion.

If you are reading this book and you have not graduated yet, please don't get discouraged; just know the obstacle you will face. It's better for me to tell you this now before you go out in the workforce with the attitude I had, thinking I was going to have it easy.

After I left Dobbs Reformatory School, I started working at Nova, which was the same as Dobbs School, working with juveniles who were too young to go to prison. I worked there for about seven months; three months were full time *without* benefits. I was upset because I had a degree in Criminal Justice and the company had full-time positions *with* benefits and other people without degrees or a criminal justice background were getting hired.

After careful consideration, it didn't bother me that the person got the job, because I knew he/she had been with the company for a while. I took into consideration the fact that they'd worked there longer than I, and had the work experience, therefore, making them more deserving of the job.

I spoke to my supervisor who was black. I believe most black people are placed in supervisory positions only to hinder other blacks. This way, whites can't say, 'Blacks are not being discriminated against because a *black* supervisor is the one that didn't hire you.'

That's the oldest trick in the book. I must admit that some black people keep themselves from getting a job because they come to interviews not speaking proper English, using slang, and not being dressed or groomed appropriately.

The world should be fair in this area specifically jobs, but it's not. I remember going to a job interview with my suit on and everything in tact , another guy was there for the interview; he just happened to be white. Even though the white guy wasn't dressed appropriately, he got the job. The fact is, he was white and probably knew someone in the company. Blacks must realize that they can't do the same thing as the white person and get away with it.

I must admit that some black supervisors don't even know they are being used to keep their race down. Some black supervisors will hire a white person for the job faster than they would their own people, who are *more qualified*. Know that this does not apply to all black supervisors.

I went to my supervisor and asked her, "Why are you hiring people off the street without any experience in Criminal Justice? You know they are scared as hell when those kids start fighting and jumping on the teachers; then I have to come over and straighten things out."

She couldn't give me an answer. She got mad at me for asking her the question. I told her what I was going to do when this happens again. When I told her I would go to her boss who was white and file a complaint, a job came open the next week and she *still* hired a person with no experience.

I went to her supervisor, which I didn't want to do considering how white people use us against each other. I explained what was going on. Her supervisor said, "Mr. Jones, I have only heard great things about you. I thought you were already a full time employee with benefits. We can't afford to lose you, because the kids listen to you. With your background you will make a great supervisor."

That white lady hired me on the spot. I worked with that Reformatory School for about three months…I knew I could get a better job. The job paid well, but I knew with my background, I could go further in life.

In 1985, my brother Terry Jones got hired with the District of Columbia (D.C.) Department of Corrections in Lorton, Virginia, which is located thirty miles outside of Washington, D.C. The District of Columbia's prisons are in Lorton, Virginia, where there is land to build prisons.

Lorton is a prison unlike most; it is broken down into seven prisons within a three-mile radius. There are Youth Center 1 and Youth Center 2, Occoquan 1, Occoquan 2, and Occoquan 3. Maximum Security, Minimum Security and of course Big Lorton, (proper name…Central Facility), is where the worst of the worst are housed. Big Lorton is like a city inside a prison.

Things weren't going like I wanted them to go after I left Nova (Reformatory School). I applied for other jobs and still wasn't satisfied. For a while I worked as a substitute teacher at the school where my uncle was principal.

I really didn't want to leave North Carolina to go work at Lorton because I had a girlfriend and my children (my oldest who was six years old, my daughter who was one year old; my youngest son wasn't born yet), but I kept entertaining the thought about Lorton.

With my background and experience I couldn't even get a job at North Carolina Department of Corrections. I put in an application to work at Lorton and a week later I received a call asking me to come in for a physical, by now it was January 1987.

When I came back from taking the physical, I got a call saying I would be in the next training class within the first week of February. A week before I was supposed to report to training, I told them I couldn't make it because I had an emergency in the family.

I lied to them about having an emergency in the family because I was hoping that North Carolina Department of Corrections would hire me. The institution gave me another reporting date of March 31, 1987. I knew I would have a job that I wanted so that I wouldn't have to leave North Carolina with the family. I didn't want to expose them to the D.C. atmosphere even though I could have stayed in Virginia.

As the weeks were approaching for me to report, time was running out. I decided to go to D.C. by myself and leave the family behind. My mindset was to get a year's worth of experience and move back. Working at Lorton, I received all of the experience I would ever need for the rest of my life.

I was working at a prison where only certain type of people survived. I had just been shot in March of 1986, and I was of the opinion that I would never let anyone hurt me again, a 'take no prisoners' attitude. A person couldn't even get close to me without me telling them, "You are invading my space!" This mentality assisted in my survival at Lorton.

The time had arrived that would change my life forever.

On March 31, 1987, I arrived in D.C. where half of my family was located and where I used to work at different jobs during the summer when I was in college. My mother and her three sisters had been living there since the early 60's, in addition to a host of first cousins, uncles and friends. It was an area that I was very familiar with…like a second home and a beautiful city.

I reported to training at Blue Plains Training Center located in Southeast D.C., which at the time had a reputation of being the worst area in D.C. It is located across the street from the Navy Yard.

When I reported to training I looked into some of the trainee's eyes and knew they shouldn't be there. I could look at some of the trainees and tell they were putting on a front; trying to be tough. As for me I felt comfortable with myself; ninety-five percent of the trainees were from D.C.

They would ask, "Where are you from, Jones?" "North Carolina"…

"Oh, you are from the south; from the country."

"You must have never left D.C., because you don't know what country is and as far as being from the south, D.C. is the south, until you cross the Mason Dixon line." I wasn't ashamed of where I was from but I had to put some people in their places by educating them in geography.

After the six-week training was over, it was lotto time. Lotto time was when the coordinator would place us at one of the seven institutions for training. They would give us a chance to select which institution we wanted to work. Most people didn't want to work at Big Lorton.

The Training Coordinator knew people didn't want to work at this prison. There were so many horror stories; sad to say the horror stories about this prison were true.

The Training Coordinator had to place us where the need was greatest. I could see the fear in some people's eyes about being sent to this prison. I took some of the pressure off of some people by volunteering to work at Big Lorton (Central Facility). By this time everyone had gotten to know and really like me and wanted to work with me. There were only two more people that volunteered to work; others were *forced* to go work there.

I felt sorry for them; I don't like seeing people afraid. The people who were *forced* to work at Big Lorton quit after being there for two weeks. I guess they didn't lose any money because we got paid while we were in training. I, on the other hand was ready to work because I wanted the overtime and the shift differential pay.

I had already gotten the scoop that people called in sick everyday, and they locked the institution down until they could get someone to work the overtime. Sometimes seventeen people would call in sick in one day. My first nine months at Lorton, I'd already made at least twenty thousand dollars in overtime.

CHAPTER 2

My First Day at Work

My first day actually working at Lorton was the second week in May 1987 on the 7:30 a.m. to 4:00 p.m. shift. I had to report to roll call. The reason the institution had roll call is because the supervisor would give us our assignments, informing us of which post we would be working.

I remember Lieutenant Hayes, a short lieutenant that looked like he had been through the ringer.

I remember him introducing the new assigned probationary officer...

"Garry Jones, front and center," he called. I knew this guy had a military background because of the language he used. I stepped out of the roll call lineup with a smile on my face.

It wasn't a smile because I was happy or anything. Most people don't know that I have a natural smile even when I'm mad.

Lieutenant Hayes said, "Why do you have that smile on your face?" I didn't think I had to answer his question and I didn't. He said, "Jones, you are not going to make it at Lorton." I didn't say anything, I just went back into formation but I was saying to myself, "Fuck you."

He proceeded to call the other probationary officers, "Front and center!" They walked up in front with a stone face. I guess after they heard what he said to me they didn't dare smile.

The sad thing about the whole situation is the other probationary officers let Lieutenant Hayes intimidate them and they *lost* who they were as people. The worst thing you can do when you work at a prison is to act bad (hard) when you're not. Inmates pick up on that real quickly. They call that type of acting, "fronting."

I never allowed anyone to change me from whom I really was, because I was always secure with the person I am inside. I can be beating your ass and smiling at the same time and not even know that I'm smiling. I remember when I would go to the inmate dining hall to monitor the inmates, they would always have a trick up their sleeve.

Inmates love to try the new officers. They try to put fear in their hearts. They would break a rule right in front of your face just to see if you are going to be afraid to step to them. I still had the same smile on my face while everyone else was trying to look serious. The fact that I had the smile on my face made the inmates feel they could try me.

One inmate came in and went right in front of the line. I politely went over to him and told him he needed to go to the back of the line. The inmate turned around and said, "I was already here!" The other inmates in line were cheering him on and saying, "Yeah, rookie, he was already in line!"

I turned and said, "Well, he is going to the back of the line before he gets anything to eat." He hesitated and stared me down as if I was going to back down.

He said, "I'm not going anywhere"... "Oh, you are going to the back"... "Fuck you, rookie!"

Before I knew it, I told him, "Turn around!" I slapped those handcuffs on him so fast that it made both of our heads spin.

I didn't stoop to his level. I took the inmate to the lieutenants' office and wrote him an incident report, which is issued when someone violates the rules and regulations.

I remember Lieutenant Hayes saying, "We don't write inmates up for disrespect to a staff member. This is a penitentiary, and inmates are going to try you like that."

"Charge him with 'disobeying an order of a staff member for not going to the back of the line.'"

Lieutenant Hayes didn't know I really wanted to curse the inmate back, but I refused to drop to the inmate's level. I went back to the mainline and the rest of the rookies (new officers on the job), were allowing inmates to jump in line in front of other inmates, even though the others had been waiting twenty minutes to eat. The rookies and the seasoned officers would turn their heads if they saw inmates jump in front of another inmate.

I realized the seasoned officers were afraid like the rookies. In order to maintain order in an institution, you have to first establish order and they expect the officers to do their jobs.

A die hard inmate is never going to go tell another staff what an inmate had done, because that is called, 'snitching,' and people get beat to death for snitching. Not too long after the mainline I had to respond to a fight; take a guess at what caused the fight… one inmate jumped in front of another inmate in the mainline. This is why it is important to follow the rules and regulations.

During my first year at Lorton, it was definitely living up to its reputation, and everyday that I worked I was gaining respect. An inmate doesn't have to like you, but if you do your job and talk to them in a respectful way you get respect.

There were times when I would curse an inmate out.

When the inmate would curse me out, I wouldn't lock him up because I had crossed the line and I knew I had crossed the line, but most of the time when I used profanity towards an inmate it was all in fun and joking.

You can't use profanity with an inmate one day and then the next day when he uses profanity towards you, you want to lock him up. That's how you lose your respect because once you gain that respect from an inmate, they are not going to use profanity towards you in front of your peers, they will respect that you have a job to do.

Usually when I had to establish order and an inmate got out of line (disorderly), I would put him back in line and never hold that against him. Even when I fought an inmate I did what I had to do to protect myself and never used excessive force.

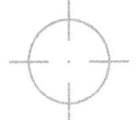

CHAPTER 3

My First Fight as a Rookie

I remember having my first fight at Lorton. It was hot, and the canteen truck had rolled in the institution. Normally rookies did not work that post. But after a couple of months at Lorton I was working posts where senior officers were supposed to work. It's dangerous to put an officer in a vital post if they were afraid; this could get an officer killed or get an inmate killed.

Wherever I worked, some inmates would say, "Why do you have to be the one work this post? I'm surprised they let you work this post. Rookies don't work this post."

Some inmates know everything about the institution and how it's supposed to run. Most of the time they know more than the staff. Even though the inmates were talking smack, I knew most of the inmates were happy I was working the canteen post because they knew if I saw someone jumping line, I would order them to go to the back.

Normally two officers worked the canteen post, because Big Lorton had over nineteen hundred inmates, and the canteen comes only twice a week. The canteen truck was a 16-wheeler truck with everything from potato chips to hygiene items. Sometimes the people who were working the canteen truck would request that *certain* staff work that post (for fear the inmates may get out of hand); obviously the supervisor thought I could handle it.

When I worked that post, it was just like rolling dice. I would keep a mental note of who jumped line and wait right before they were getting ready to purchase their items and tell them to go to the back of the line. Then they would say, "I didn't jump the line, Jones."

I would say, "I know you didn't *just* jump the line, you jumped it *twenty minutes ago*."

A lot of inmates didn't want to take that chance. I must admit inmates got over on me, but not that often.

I remember seeing an inmate getting his canteen, he hadn't jumped the line but after he gave the staff his canteen card, he tried to get canteen for someone else. An inmate can't purchase canteen for others. I walked up with the intentions of letting him keep the canteen he'd purchased, but I took the other person's canteen sheet and card. The inmate snatched the canteen sheet out of my hands…he made one mistake. When he snatched the canteen sheet out of my hand, he scratched me and I snapped.

I hit him in the face and picked him up over my shoulder to carry him out in the middle of the yard, because I couldn't use my radio for help. Most of the time when there was a fight, inmates would gather around, so that none of the other officers could see the officer fighting. That's when the inmates start kicking the officer, and he or she does not know which inmate did it.

After I got the inmate in the middle of the yard, I started wearing his ass out until the officers came over and broke it up. Hitting a staff member is serious business; an inmate can get five extra years added to their sentence.

When the officers came over to take the inmate to the hole or lock-up, the major wanted to see the inmate and wanted to know if I was okay. I told the officers to tell the major I would be in his office in a few minutes. Normally, I wouldn't handle a fight like I did that time. I usually call for backup when I know something is getting ready to jump off, but when the inmate hit me, I reacted quickly. I didn't want to go and do all the paperwork that I was supposed to do (for the incident), because I wanted to cool off first.

After the fight, my mind went back to the night I got shot. When I went back to the canteen truck, there was no talking among the inmates. They even straightened up the line. One of the inmates did say, "Shorty, you are pretty good with your hands, but if you would have done me like that I would have knocked your country ass out."

I called the inmate out of line and said, "Come on. Let's get it over with since you are talking all of that smack."

The inmate refused to get out of line; immediately he lost his respect, not from me, but from other inmates. When inmates are in a penitentiary setting, it's important for him to keep his word and when they talk smack to an officer, and don't back it up, they lose respect from their peers because they know that inmate is 'all mouth and no action.'

I guess that inmate who said he would have knocked me out didn't think I would come back and say, "Come on and let's get it over with." The best thing he could have done was kept his mouth closed just like the rest of the inmates. Word got out quick that Jones could fight, this spread all over Lorton, even at the other prisons at Lorton.

I heard a page come across the radio, "Officer Jones, report to the Major's office."

Another officer came to relieve me. When I reported to the Major's office, he asked if I had been checked at the hospital. I told him I didn't feel the need to.

He said, "Forget about the hospital, come in the office and we'll deal with the hospital later."

When I came to one of the head men's office, Lieutenant Hayes and another guy were there and the inmate was crying. One of them said, "Jones, close the door."

"Did you hit my officer?"

The inmate said, "It was a mistake. I was trying to take something out of his hands, but I made a mistake and hit his hand."

One of the head men said, "You must be out of your mind to hit a big guy like Jones," then he hauled off and slapped the inmate... "Do you know why I hit you?"

"No."

"Because you are stupid to hit my officer," then he slapped the inmate again.

"Do you know why I slapped you," the inmate was crying...

"No"…

"Because you are crazy to hit an officer like Jones."

Then another one of them slapped the inmate and said, "Do you know why I slapped you," the inmate was crying really hard… "I wouldn't even go against Jones myself."

Then the other head man said, "Jones go ahead and take care of him."

I told him, "I whipped him on the yard. I don't need to do anymore damage, as far as I'm concerned, it's over."

"Go ahead and process the inmate for an assault on a staff member." I did the paperwork and then he said, "Jones, take the inmate to the hole!"

Lieutenant Hayes said, "No, let him go back on the compound or the yard!" The inmate started crying, saying he didn't want to go back to the yard.

They were teasing the inmate, because they knew we couldn't put an inmate back on the yard after he assaulted an officer or committed a major violation. The reason the inmate didn't want to go back to the yard was because, he knew after he hit an officer he had to go to the hole and new charges would be brought against him. If that inmate would have gone back to the compound, he would have been dead within an hour because the other inmates would have known he did a lot of snitching to be able to get out of a charge for assaulting an officer.

I went to the hospital after checking the inmate into the hole (location for disciplinary inmates). The Major called me back and asked if I was going to press charges with the F.B.I.

for the inmate assaulting me. I told him that as far as I was concerned it was over.

Lieutenant Hayes called me into his office and said, "Jones, I thought you were going to be soft, but I realize you are the best rookie we ever had, but you need to wipe that smile off your face. You are still at a penitentiary."

CHAPTER 4

Guns on the Inside

I reported to work at 11:30 p.m. for the midnight shift, and when I got to roll call, I noticed there were three times the amount of staff than usual, in addition to this, the faces were not familiar. When the lieutenant started roll call, he stated, "Some snitches said inmates had guns in the laundry room and the additional officers are here because we are going to search the entire laundry room in three's until we find the weapons."

Sometimes they send officers from different institutions to do shakedowns (look for illegal items), because at times, the regular officers working at the institution become complacent and may miss seeing certain things. Someone new to the institution, sent in just for the purpose of looking for illegal contraband, can pinpoint and spot things out of the ordinary.

After roll call, some of the people reported to their regular posts, but I was one of the officers they chose to send to the laundry room for the big shakedown. The first hour of shaking down the laundry room we didn't find anything.

Around 1:15 a.m., one of the crews found a .45 automatic pistol fully loaded; from then on we found a shotgun, and three more pistols. I didn't actually find any weapons on my own, but we didn't finish shaking the laundry down until the mainline.

We found shanks (homemade knives), drugs, and anything that would cause us to think that a major fight was going to take place, not with the officers but with rival gangs. Sometimes gangs weren't the only groups that did a lot of fighting. When different religious sects got into a major altercation it would get nasty, especially with Mosaic Science Muslims groups against the Nation of Islam. It's not wise to disrespect anyone's religion; all hell breaks loose.

Before I started working with the Criminal Justice System, I never got into debates about religion. I respected people's religion, and I expect people to respect mine as well. Working in the prison system I made it a point never to discuss religion with inmates.

After mainline, we wrapped up the whole shake down, and started processing the paperwork to present to the F.B.I. Some of the inmates were hollering, "You all didn't find everything! There are plenty more weapons on this compound!"

They were right. Later, during my tenure at Lorton, it was nothing to come to work and discover that a staff member found a gun or some ammunition. I could tell by the weapons that were found, that these weren't all homemade weapons. Staff members were bringing in these weapons. The going price for bringing in weapons by a staff member was at least five thousand dollars. Drugs were the same…depending on what types of drugs were brought in. The going price for a staff member to bring the illegal items in was two to three thousand dollars.

At any prison, bringing in contraband was a money making machine for staff members. Staff could make more money bringing in contraband than their annual salary.

There was a heavy price to pay if a staff got caught bringing major contraband (illegal items) into the prison. Sometimes they lost their jobs, but if drugs and guns were involved, they lost their job and started doing time themselves, (went to prison).

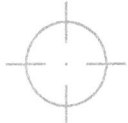

CHAPTER 5

Losing My Cool

Every now and then I would lose my cool while at work, but it took a lot for me to stoop down to a lower level of professionalism. When I worked, mainline inmates were still up to their old tricks. They would still try to jump in front of other inmates, instead of waiting their turn.

They couldn't resist the temptation of getting over on me, and I couldn't resist the temptation of catching them in the wrong. I wasn't going around looking for trouble; it seemed like trouble was finding me. It seemed as though the inmates wanted to try me. Someone was always laying in the cut to try Big J. I had so many nicknames at the institution it wasn't funny, all the way from Big J, Big Country, Smooth, and Cockstrong.

Sometimes I could sense that the inmates wanted to fight me and win. They knew if they beat me they would score some points with other inmates. I wasn't a big person but I was ripped; muscular, and to whip someone like me would get them major respect around the yard.

The inmates knew I wouldn't press charges if I ever got into an altercation with them.

The opportunity presented itself with one inmate who totally disrespected me. He looked at me, then, went straight to the front of the line. As usual I told him to go to the back of the line. I had gotten to the point that I wasn't going word for word with anyone.

The inmate and I had a small altercation, but he went to the back of the line. After he finished eating, the same inmate came to me and asked me if I was 'ready.'

"Ready for what," I said.

"I'm ready to whip your big ass."

The inmate was about five feet four inches tall and he was ripped more than I was.

"Yeah, I'm ready, but let's take this somewhere else. Follow me."

He said, "No let's do it now."

I wasn't a fool. I wasn't going to strike an inmate unless they struck me, but the inmate didn't want to take the first lick.

I wasn't going to lose my job only to prove that I could whip him. I knew if the inmate struck me first I would be justified when the fight started.

"Let's go to a place alone to settle the matter."

Like a dummy he said, "You pick the place Big Country."

I took him to the control center. I told the control center officer, 'I needed the keys to the shakedown room because I need to do a strip search of an inmate.'

After receiving the keys from the control center officer, I took the inmate to the shakedown area. When I got the inmate inside of the shakedown area I locked the door, and moved the desk out of the way and commenced beating his ass. He got a couple of licks in my face but that was all.

The inmate was shorter than me; I could tell when we were fighting, he would try to go low on me and grab my legs. What he was trying to do was get me in one of those wrestling moves, but I was too strong for him. During the fight when both of us locked up, meaning both of us grabbed each other in the center of our bodies; I was able to use my strength to lift the inmate over my shoulder and take him to the ground. I didn't just take him to the ground. I took him to the ground with all the force that I had, and when I body slammed him he had no way of breaking the fall because his hands were around my chest. That wrestling move was called the 'Bear Hug.'

Nevertheless, when the inmate hit the ground, he screamed, and my mind went immediately back to the night I had gotten shot. I started wearing his face out with my fist. With all the commotion going on, an officer asked, "Is everything okay," but I didn't reply. I could hear the officer trying to get in the door, but it was locked. The officer ran to control, got the emergency keys, and called for all available staff to report to the shakedown room.

When the officer came to the shakedown room I was still beating the inmate. They pulled me off the inmate, and the inmate couldn't do anything but ball up in a fetal position and hold his head crying. When the investigation was conducted I told the lieutenant, "When I asked the inmate to take off his clothes (for the strip search), he took a swing at me." The investigation revealed that the inmate said he was in debt, and if he didn't come up with the money he was going to be killed. He told the lieutenant that he needed a way to get locked up. He said, "Jones didn't fall for the bait of fighting him in the mainline." The inmate admitted to starting the whole fight, but he couldn't go back on the yard. He needed to be transferred to another institution. The lieutenant told him that he had picked the wrong officer to fight. The inmate was later transferred to another institution.

CHAPTER 6

Working the Visitation Room

The visitation room was an area where the inmates' family came to visit them. Often family members brought in drugs. The inmates would also try to get their groove on (have sex) when an officer was not looking.

The only time the inmate was allowed to kiss their spouse was when they greeted each other at the beginning of the visit, and when the visit was over. I was working in the visitation room, of which I took seriously. The reason I took it so seriously was because often inmates would have their hands in their visitor's panties or they were getting oral sex with their spouse or girlfriends.

Some of the inmates didn't give a damn about respect. They knew they could get away with having sex with their visitor when certain officers were working, but not with me. I could care less about the inmate not respecting me in the visiting room, but what I couldn't deal with was the elderly and the kids seeing the inmates having sex. That burned me up inside.

Some of the officers would often turn their heads, because they were afraid to tell the inmate to stop or suspend the visit. I didn't have a problem suspending an inmate's visit when they engaged in sex. These inmates did not care about the fact that other visitors were looking at them.

I remember when a call came across the walkie-talkie, "All available staff, report to the phone room!" There were so many areas in Lorton that needed attention. I ran from the visiting room, to the phone room where two inmates were fighting.

The fight started because the corporal didn't do his job in monitoring the time the inmate spent on the phone. If an inmate went over his allotted time; the operator would cut the phones off at a certain time. The inmates had to first sign up during the week to make a phone call, and on the weekends, was when inmates were able to make long distance calls. The inmates were limited to only five minutes on the phone, and if the officer allowed the inmate to go over, it meant at the end of the phone period someone would not get a chance to make their call and you knew right then a fight was going to break out.

I asked the corporal if he wanted me to take the inmates to the hole (lock up). The inmates told the corporal that they were playing not fighting. Any fool could see that these two inmates were fighting. Because the corporal was being too friendly with some of the inmates, he decided to let them go back to their units, which was against policy. Even if the inmates *were* playing, they should have been taken to lock up just in case they were lying. This would give the inmates a chance to cool off if indeed there was a fight.

I wasn't on probation anymore, but the corporal had more rank than I did so I couldn't overturn his decision. After all the inmates left the phone room, I spoke with him about the situation for about ten minutes. This guy was jealous of me because he had been at Lorton a long time and couldn't advance. I had been at Lorton for only a year and handled some of the toughest situations *by myself*. I was on my way to the top in rank.

It was only a matter of time that I would get promoted.

When I was on my way back to my assigned post at the visiting room, I'd seen and heard a loud gathering on the North Walk (a section of the prison). I heard someone calling out numbers like, "number two, number seven," and every time I heard a number being called, I would hear someone screaming.

When I went to investigate the situation, I could see other inmates stabbing this one inmate. When the other inmates looked up, they saw me and said, "Don't come over here or you can get some of this too!"

Inmates don't stab another inmate in front of a staff member. Usually if a staff member comes over, they will stop, or they will get the inmate in a blind spot, (a place where the officer working in the tower can't see the inmate stabbing). This group did not do this. They didn't stop stabbing the inmate when they saw me. These inmates intended to kill this guy.

As I was getting ready to call control on my walkie-talkie, I heard control say, "All available units report to the hollow (another section of the prison)!" There were two things going on at one time. The inmates had it set up like that. They planned to have a fight going on in the hollow, so that they could divert the attention from the North Walk section of the prison where they were stabbing this inmate. It was the only chance that I happened to be going back to my post in the visiting room and heard the screaming.

I told control that I had a situation over on the North Walk. The control center officer said, "Jones, go ahead and handle what you have."

"I can't handle the situation on my own…I need back up!"

Inmates were stabbing to kill and had every intention of coming after me next. I was in a hostile situation.

I told control, "Call the infirmary and send someone over with a stretcher because I have a stabbing in progress!" "Be patient, Jones"…

I forgot which tower I called to cover me as I kept approaching the stabbing but the tower said, "Jones, if they come after you run towards the Administration Building and I will have you in sight. I will fire the weapon if they attack you."

Me On Tower Duty

I was in a hostile situation by myself. Normally inmates don't stab other inmates in front of staff, because they don't want to be identified. I took five more steps towards the stabbing. That's when I identified three inmates; two of the inmates were the inmates that had just finished fighting in the phone room. I made eye contact with the inmate that had been stabbed, by this time, everyone decided to finally scatter.

I went over to check him out and he kept saying, "Please don't let me die."

I called control. "I still need back up and a stretcher; and lock down the yard!"

"We can't lock the yard down because we have another fight in progress!"

In ten minutes someone finally brought a stretcher and the inmate was taken to the infirmary; then later transported to D.C. General Hospital. When everything came under control, officers and lieutenants came over to lock up the suspects. We went in every unit on the North Walk; as we walked through the unit, I identified the inmates in the area of the stabbing; they were being taken out of the unit to lock up.

We were also looking for the weapons. In one of the units there were people in the shower, and as they came out of the shower, I identified two more inmates involved in the stabbing as well as the inmates that were involved in the fight in the phone room.

While the officers were taking the inmates out of the unit, a cat was walking around with bloody paws. Cats usually kept the mice away; the inmates fed the cats and kept them for pets. When I started looking down I followed the bloody paws; the bloody paws guided me to a bunk. When I got to the bunk, I saw a shank under it. I looked at the name and number on the bunk. That bunk belonged to the same inmate that I saw fighting in the phone room but he had already been identified by me, and taken to lock-up.

After the investigation was over, I discovered why I was hearing inmates calling out numbers. The inmates belonged to a gang and numbers identified them. After the inmates in the phone room got back to their units they were finishing up the fight they had originally been involved in. One of the inmates belonged to a gang, and when he went to get his boys, they cornered the one inmate who was involved in the first fight.

Whenever an inmate called out a number, the inmate that was assigned that particular number would step up and stab the inmate that had been cornered. The inmate who was being stabbed didn't know where the next stabbing was coming from. If he got stabbed in the front of his body, another inmate would stab him from the side.

The next day I was recognized in roll call by Lieutenant Hayes with a Letter of Commendation for not putting myself in a hostile situation, but having sense enough to take mental notes of some of the inmates involved in the altercation and identifying them. My popularity went up with the staff. I was being assigned to sergeant in charge of a post. This would later end, after I received a phone call from the North Carolina Department of Corrections to work for them.

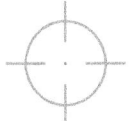

CHAPTER 7

My Last Fight at Lorton

In July of 1988, I was assigned to work in the lock-up unit. The lock-up unit required at least seven staff members to work on that post. The lock-up unit was dark and gloomy as if it was built in the 1920's, and had one big steel door where inmates were brought in when they got into trouble.

Lorton was an old institution. It didn't have air conditioning. It was okay to work the lock-up in the wintertime, because the lock-up unit had heat, but the summer, was a different story. This particular day it was over one hundred degrees and we had those big giant industrial fans running to cool things off.

The Unit Disciplinary Team was inside the lock-up in another room listening to inmates who had incident reports (shots). The proper protocol was to go to the cell and get inmates for the unit team where their incidents reports could be heard. Three officers would go to the cell and tell the inmate to come forward, turn around and be cuffed.

The sergeant would call control for them to open certain cells. We would bring the inmate to the unit disciplinary team, they would then tell us to get other inmates ready to be called for their incident reports to be heard. We would go back and get those inmates and bring them up front to sit on the bench. I asked the sergeant if I could open the steel door.

"Yes," he said.

When the steel door opened, there was a big screen door where you could see the yard or compound. The inmates could be seen moving around and doing their regular routine. I was standing in front of the screen door basically daydreaming about what I was going to do when I went back to North Carolina. All of

Suddenly an inmate came and kicked the trash can over that was placed in front of the lock-up.

I told the inmate to pick up the trash can as well as the trash. I knew the inmate. I'd had plenty of conversations with him; he never gave me any trouble. Sometimes when an inmate is serving a lot of time, it gets the best of them, especially when they have served ten years and still have twenty more years to go before they are released, if not, a life sentence. I asked the inmate a second time to pick up the trash.

He said, "Fuck you, Jones!"

"I am going to ask you one more time to pick up the trash can and if you don't, you are going to lock-up where I am working."

The inmate disobeyed my order. When the inmate didn't comply with my orders the third time, I opened the screen door and told him to come in so I could talk to him. I could tell something was bothering him because he never disrespected me. When he came into the lock-up unit, I asked him what was going on.

"Nothing is going on. It was just another hot day at Lorton."

"Go back outside and pick up the trash and the trash can."

"I'm not going to do it."

"Give me your DCDC."

The DCDC was an inmate number to identify who he was.

The inmate said, "I know you are not going to write me a shot for this, Jones."

I didn't have any intentions on writing the inmate a shot, but he wasn't going to refuse my order and not pick up the trash and the trash can.

He said, "If you are going to lock me up I will give you something to lock me up over," before he could get the last word out of his mouth, he hit me in the face with a closed fist and pushed me against the wall.

I bounced off the wall and hit the inmate with at least five punches and I commenced to picking him up and body slamming him on the hard concrete. The sergeant pushed the panic button and officers started responding to the lock-up unit. It became a brawl. The inmates sitting on the bench came over even though they weren't handcuffed by the ankles and started stomping me in the back of the head, but I was still whipping the inmates' ass; my mind kept going back to the night I had gotten shot in the club. I couldn't stop punching the inmate.

The officers were still trying to gain control over the situation. The inmates in the yard came over and were peeping inside the lock-up unit to find out what was going on. One of the inmates that peeped in realized I was beating his brother. He came over because someone in the yard went to his unit and told him that Jones just took his brother inside of lock-up.

After order was restored, I was bleeding from the mouth and the back of my neck was hurting. My shirt was covered with blood.

One of the officers said, "Someone take the inmate to the infirmary."

"No! Jones will be seen by the doctors before an inmate gets seen," said Lieutenant Hayes.

When I left the lock-up to go get treatment, the inmates' brother started walking towards me very fast. I knew what he was coming to do, but my right arm was hurting and the only thing I could do was swing at him before he jumped on me, but some officers interfered and broke up a fight that was about to happen between me and the inmate's brother.

I got treated at the infirmary, but the inmate I had been fighting had gotten hurt very badly. They had to transport him to D.C. General Hospital for treatment.

CHAPTER 8

Leaving Lorton

Before I left Lorton, there were so many staff members asking me not to leave, they told me they would give me a counseling position or promote me to a lieutenant. I had to be a corporal and then a sergeant before I got promoted to a lieutenant. The staff at Lorton was doing everything they could to entice me to stay.

My mind was made up; I was going back to North Carolina to work with the North Carolina Department of Corrections, and begin taking classes towards my Master's Degree.

Needless to say, I went to work and never went back to school to earn my Master's Degree in Criminal Justice. My last day at work my home girl Captain Michelle Giles , who was the Training Coordinator, supported my move although she really didn't want me to go back to North Carolina. She didn't want me to leave, because I was doing such a good job at Lorton.

When I reported to roll call they had a party for me, presented gifts, and asked me to say some departing words. I'm never at a loss for words, so I gave a small speech, and my tenure at Lorton was over. I could write three books about Lorton but I only highlighted the things that I felt would interest my readers. In this book, I didn't get into a lot of other things, such as the escapes I prevented.

CHAPTER 9

Triangle Correctional Institution

I finally left Lorton and returned to North Carolina. I received the experience I needed in order to deal with what was to come later on in my life. I didn't actually go back to my hometown of Kinston, North Carolina. Instead, I resided in Raleigh, North Carolina. My girlfriend and my children were still living in Kinston, one hour and twenty minutes away; I didn't move them with me, because I didn't plan on being in Raleigh very long.

In August 1988, I began my career with Triangle Correctional Institution. Up to this point in my life, I had never heard of Triangle Correctional Institution.

While working in Lorton (in D.C.), my Aunt Mavis Jones, would always keep a copy of my resume, to assist me with getting a job in corrections that was closer to home. She would check for job openings in corrections, and she would send my application to different institutions.

I can recall being in Washington D.C., receiving calls from different places asking me to set up interviews with them. I went to North Carolina to interview with Wayne Correctional Institution. I think it was for the job as a Drug Treatment Rehabilitation Specialist. I was always qualified, but politics played a major role with me not getting the job.

I would always get back on the highway pissed off saying to myself, 'I have the education and experience and still can't get hired in my own state.' This made me think about Jesus when he said, "A prophet will not be accepted in his hometown." Of course I'm not calling myself a prophet. It's just that no one would accept me in my home state.

I remember getting this call from Triangle Correctional Institution. I'd heard of the other institutions that called me for an interview, but as I mentioned earlier, I had never heard of Triangle Correctional Institution.

The party on the other line said, "Are you Garry Jones?"

"Yes."

"Could you come in tomorrow morning for an interview?"

"Have you taken out the time to see where I am located?"

She said, "You are in Washington, D.C." I couldn't come for the interview unless I got at least a week's advance notice. I told the lady my days off, and told her to set the interview according to my days off. It was very unprofessional for these people to ask me to come in exactly one day before the interview, knowing I lived in another state. Could they have been afraid of my education and experience? Did they have someone else in mind for the job, and the fact that my educational background and experience put the person they had in mind for the job in jeopardy? Is that why they called me the day before the interview knowing I was living in another state?

They knew it was impossible for me to drive there the next day while I was working. When a person has been through the things I'd been through, questions like that tend to pop up in your mind. I was a threat to the person they wanted to give the job to. I'm glad Warden Glenn Combs, was professional. It didn't hurt that our birthdays were on the same day...January 25th.

I remember going to Triangle for the interview. When Mr. Combs interviewed me I could tell that he was impressed. After the interview I returned to D.C. with a good feeling that I had that job. I was smiling from ear to ear on the highway driving my Nissan Sentra back to the District.

When I arrived home, I checked the answering machine and just like I thought, someone in personnel asked me to call Triangle Correctional Institution as soon as possible. Being that it was late when I arrived, I said to myself, 'I'll call tomorrow.' The next morning when I called, I was told I had the job as a correctional officer. The lady I spoke with asked if I could start the job one week later. I told her, "No!" I remember being furious when she asked if I could start the following week.

That airhead knew I was staying in the District, when you are moving you have to relocate, organize things and get settled. I wanted to give my old job a two-week notice that I was leaving. I called and spoke with Warden Combs. I thanked him for hiring me and explained to him that I wanted to give my job a two-week notice before I come to Triangle. He said, "Take your time and do what you have to do."

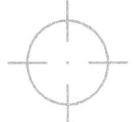

CHAPTER 10

The First Day on the Job

The first day on the job I had to go to the clothing building and get fitted for my uniform. The inmates fit the officers for their uniforms. They already knew who I was, and where I was coming from.

They said, "You are the guy from Lorton, aren't you?" I said, "Yes sir, I am."

The inmate was surprised that I replied to him with, 'Yes sir.' We had some small talk, and before I left the clothing room the inmate said, "Man coming from Lorton to Triangle is day and

47

night. You might get bored here, because this place is a processing unit for inmates that are going to other institutions to do their time."

The inmate was right. I got bored real quick. I was treated with respect, most of the time it's like that wherever I go because I live by the golden rule, "Do unto others as you would have them do unto you."

I was happy to be close to my girlfriend and kids, but at the same time I had a problem dealing with the slow pace at Triangle. I knew I wasn't going to be at Triangle long, but I didn't want to disappoint Mr. Combs because he had given me a chance. Later on when I got off work I came home to tell my aunt about the job, she asked me to check my mail.

When I checked my mail, it was a letter from the Federal Correctional Institution Butner, located in Butner, North Carolina. When I opened up the mail, the letter stated, I had to come to Butner, North Carolina the next day and take my physical. I wanted to work for the federal government but this wasn't professional at all, (another short notice for a new job).

I called Butner the next morning and told them I had just gotten the letter. I asked them if I could come the next day (not the day they indicated in the letter) and take the physical.

They said, "No."

I explained to them that I had to take off work to come, and that was something I didn't want to do considering I'd been working at Triangle for only one day. Butner was only an hour away from Raleigh, North Carolina.

The personnel at Butner weren't trying to work with me so I said forget it, take me off your list and call someone else.

I did things the professional, responsible way, and I couldn't disappoint Mr. Combs because he saw the potential in me. I had made friends with some of the officers at Triangle.

We would go out and get a drink when we got off work and tell war stories. All the guys I hung around were from the military. Most people that work at correctional facilities have military backgrounds. These guys would always want to hear my war stories at Lorton because Lorton had a reputation… if you survived working at Lorton, you could survive working anywhere and they were right.

It took me a long time to come down from the fast pace at Lorton to the slow pace at Triangle. As a matter of fact even today, I haven't had a challenge at any job that could come close to working at Lorton.

I came to realize while working at Triangle there would always be some 'haters.' Haters are people who hate you for no reason. They hate you because of the respect you command with staff and other inmates.

What the staff didn't realize was wherever I worked I was always myself; I never tried to put on a front for anyone. I am comfortable with the person I am. The biggest mistake that a person makes when working at a correctional facility is they think they have to have that tough man or woman mentality. I refused to be anybody other than who God made me to be. I could care less where I worked; putting on a front was something I wasn't going to do. I felt very secure with whom I was.

My first fight at Triangle was not with an inmate, but with a staff member; because they felt I was a rookie, they thought they could use their authority to demand that I follow their orders. I didn't have problems with following orders, but I did have a problem with the way people talked to me. If they didn't respect me then they had an issue, because I didn't have a problem putting them in their place.

I can recall the fight with the staff member like it was yesterday. When it was count time, the officer that had outranked me asked me to count with him. What I mean by this is, at any institution a count was conducted at least four times during a twenty-four hour period.

I know in the federal system, we had to conduct a count of the inmates at least five times. The reason we counted the inmates so often, was to ensure every inmate was accounted for. If an inmate was out of place we had to find out where they were. If we couldn't account for them, then we knew someone had escaped.

Every officer is supposed to count their assigned unit, and we had to count in pairs. One officer would go down the aisle and count, while the other remained behind to cover for him. After one officer counted, the officer that covered, would go down and count. After the count, both would compare counts to ensure both came up with the same number. If we didn't come up with the same number we had to recount. I remember counting with this one officer; he would just walk the aisle as if he was counting and after the count, he would ask me what I came up with. I knew he wasn't counting the inmates. He would walk down that aisle so fast and count both sides, as if he were the world's greatest counter. When we (officers) count we have to take our time, because we have to look, and make sure the inmate is still breathing especially if we were working the midnight shift.

If officers didn't take anything else seriously, we had to take the count seriously. Our job was to make sure we accounted for the inmates and to ensure they didn't escape where they could go out, and be a danger to the public. Basically, the only duty, correctional officers' have, is to babysit.

As the count went on in every unit, the officer would ask me the same thing, "What did you come up with?"

I would say, "Let's compare counts. You show me the total of your count and I'll show you the total of my count."

As time went on, the officer became angry. His true feelings came out when it was time to count the inmates in the canteen (where food products, hygiene items, etc. are purchased).

That particular evening there were only four inmates in the canteen, and when I counted, I came up with four inmates; he came up with three inmates. He didn't mind counting the canteen inmates, there wasn't as many to count compared to the dormitories. I told him to recount. He said, "I told you I came up with three inmates."

"I came up with four inmates."

"I'm tired of you Jones!"

"I don't care about what you are tired of. If you want to know the true count, call the control center; I'll bet you there are four inmates."

What the lazy officer didn't know was that I went to the back of the canteen and saw an inmate doing inventory. I could have very well instructed that inmate to come up front to be counted, but why should I do that with only four inmates?

It wasn't like there was a dormitory full of inmates, so I let the inmate continue his job.

When the officer didn't want to call the count into the control center, he went to the back of the canteen, because one of the inmates was giving him the eye as if to say, 'we do have one more inmate in the back.' When the officer found out I was right, he was pissed. After counting the canteen inmates, we took the shortcut through the cafeteria to get to the other side of the institution in order to count one more unit. As we were going to the other side of the institution, the officer stopped and said, "I told you I was tired of you!"

He had a clipboard in his hand. In my opinion I think he accidentally hit me in the face with the clipboard. I honestly don't think that he did this intentionally, but I reacted quickly and hit him a couple of times, taking him to the ground. When I had the officer on the ground, I regained my composure and told the officer never to put his hands on me again. My mind immediately went back to the time I was fighting in the club and got shot. After I let the officer get up off the ground I asked him, "What do you want to do about this incident?" This incident could have led to both of us being fired.

Later on I was called into the sergeant's office and asked, "What went on between you and the officer in the cafeteria?"

"The officer got mad because I wanted to compare counts while we were counting."

I wasn't going to tell the sergeant what really happened.

He told the sergeant that we had an argument in the cafeteria about the count, and that I was in his face cursing at him. He didn't tell him what had really transpired. I told the sergeant he hit me and I took him to the ground. This was supposed to have been confidential between the officer and me.

When the sergeant asked him if it really happened, he told the sergeant, "Yes." This officer put the sergeant in a position that he didn't want to be in. The sergeant wanted me to lose my job, but if he reported the incident there was a possibility that both of us were going to lose our jobs. He told us to shake hands, forget about the incident and not to say anything about it.

At 10:00 p.m. I left to go home, but the homeboy stayed in the sergeant's office. On my way home I didn't feel right about the situation. I felt like I was going to be set up. At 1:00 a.m. I called the institution and informed the shift lieutenant about what happened.

He said, "I know what happened because I am writing the report as we speak. I'm glad you called back, because I received a different story from the officer and the sergeant."

The shift lieutenant told me to come to the institution and write my side of the story. I knew the cards were stacked against me, so I gave my version. I know those bastards and how they are, so I was forced to go to the warden to tell him about the incident. I told the warden the truth; he told me not to worry about it. He said when the report comes to his office he would deal with it.

The shift lieutenant that I'd called at 1:00 a.m. told me that he felt like the sergeant and the officer were lying and even though he never worked with me, he knew my character and the story that the sergeant and the officer told was different. After the investigation was over, the sergeant got suspended.

The officer and I didn't get suspended, but the officer got reprimanded. I never received anything. The sergeant just got suspended for a couple days because of the lie he told to cover up for the officer. The sergeant had been written up before for coming to work with alcohol on his breath.

Two months later I went to the warden and told him that I wanted to schedule a meeting with him. He told me to set the time and the date. I explained to him that I'm grateful that he had given me a chance to come work at his institution, and I was glad to be a correctional officer, but I wanted to do other things in life. I told him I wanted to be a program assistant, which was a case Manager for the inmates.

He stated he was glad I was trying to advance instead of just accepting what I had and being satisfied. He said he hired me because of the potential I had and he told me I shouldn't just want to settle for being a correctional officer even though nothing was wrong with being a correctional officer. Mr. Combs stated that if a program assistant (case manager) position became available, he would keep me in mind.

Two weeks later I found a note in my box about an opening for a job at another institution for a program assistant. Mr. Combs had put the memo in my box and highlighted it with a yellow marker; it stated F.Y.I. I applied for the job at Wake Correctional Institution the following week, and three weeks later I was called for an interview. Of course, I was dressed to the 'T,' and I had been brushing up on my interview skills. One of my friends, Melvin Scott gave me a book entitled Knock 'em Dead. The book goes into details on how to tighten up your interview skills, and what colors to wear when you apply for a job, depending on the season of the year.

You can bet in every job interview you will have the primary questions. Why should I hire you? Why should I hire you over the other person? What's your strongest point? What's your weakest point? I had honed in on those questions. I can't remember every question they asked me in the interview but there was one question that stood out in my mind, and I will never forget it. I was asked, "What is your strongest point?"

I can't recall verbatim but I did say, my strongest point is my ability to communicate with people from all walks of life.

I had to give them that answer because working in a prison, we encounter people from all walks of life and cultures, and if we are not sensitive to other people's culture, we can make big mistakes of offending them.

I knew I had that ability to communicate with anyone. In turn the interviewer asked me, "What is your weakest point?"

I informed her that my typing abilities were not that good, but I had taken a typing course in high school, and I was familiar with the typewriter.

I think she asked the next question because she thought I was lying. If anyone knows anything about typing, the first thing they teach you are your home keys. As a matter of fact the only thing I know about typing is the home keys, and at one time I was typing with both hands, but after the course in high school, I didn't have a need to know how to type.

The interviewer asked, "Mr. Jones you said your weak point was that you didn't know how to type well..."

"Yes, you are correct."

She then asked me, "What are your home keys?" "a, s, d, f, and g then h, j, k, l, and ;(semi-colon)."

That lady turned red in the face. She was impressed with the interview. I can't say whether or not Mr. Combs made a phone call and put a word in for me, but if he did put in a good word for me, he was pleased with the way I handled the interview. I walked out of that interview waiting for them to call me and tell me I had the job. I knew I had aced the interview.

Two weeks later I received a call with the job offer, and within a month I was working at Wake Correctional Center as a program assistant (case manager). I was typing with one finger then, and I'm still typing with one finger and I still know my home keys.

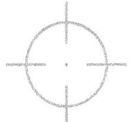

CHAPTER 11

Wake Correctional Center

I worked at Triangle Center for eleven months, and now I was working across town at Wake Correctional Center as a case manager. I was out of the uniforms, and dressed with a suit and tie on certain occasions, but most of the time I was dressed with a pair of slacks and a tie. I had embarked on a new career in Criminal Justice.

I was still in corrections, but I had a caseload, and was responsible for a lot of inmates. I had to adhere to the judge's orders for what the inmate needed to do, once they arrived at prison. If an inmate didn't have a GED, I had to make sure the inmate was enrolled in the GED classes.

After ninety days of incarceration the inmate had to be enrolled in a class. If the inmate committed a drug related crime, I had to ensure that he got some type of drug treatment. Most of the time I was tied to my desk. I didn't receive any training for my new position. I had to look and learn. Depending on whom you are working with, you can get the correct hands-on training or learn the shortcut.

I had one supervisor that showed me both the shortcut to doing things and/or the long or correct way of doing things. Nevertheless, I had a choice. Some of the staff members wouldn't show the new staff anything. I was working in the office with Martin; he was a case manager also. Both of us graduated from North Carolina Central University. It's ironic, because he graduated in 1985 and I graduated in 1986, but we never crossed paths while we were in college.

Martin was a born again Christian, but he was so smooth with the way he talked with you, so as not to offend you if you weren't a Christian. He led the life, without beating you on the head with the Bible. Martin and I got along very well. We had different supervisors, but Martin showed me the in's and out's of the job. Even with this being the case, I still had to learn a lot of things on my own. I could tell he didn't want me to fail.

We only had one radio in the office, and Martin would listen to a gospel station at a certain time. I respected that, but he also respected the fact that I wanted to listen to R&B, so we worked it out where he would listen to gospel at a certain time, and I would listen to R&B at a certain time. We had different schedules. On the days I would come in for the 2:00 p.m. shift to 10:00 p.m. shift, he would come in at 8:00 a.m. to 4:00 p.m.

On Fridays, both of us worked 8:00 a.m. to 4:00 p.m. For the first couple of months I would come in on Saturdays, because I was learning things on my own, not to mention the office was quiet. I had to set up my own system and style of work that would benefit me. I would go through every inmate file I had on my caseload and decide the need of the inmate.

Of course my files were not updated, because when a new person comes in to work, a lot of the other case managers dumped their files on the new person. It wasn't easy maintaining a caseload, but nevertheless the job got done.

Normally, when an inmate first reports to the institution, they have a thirty-day review, sixty-day review, ninety-day review, six-month review and a yearly review. I would record all of the inmate's review dates, and type them out. Whenever an inmate was coming up on a review, I would let them know by sending them a, 'Request to See Staff Memo,' letting them know what time to meet me in my office.

I had all of the inmate's names in alphabetical order, along with when we were scheduled to meet. It was hard getting all of this information recorded, but in the long run, it was easy to keep track of every inmate on my caseload. Most inmates were excited to see me in person, because they hadn't seen their case manager. A lot of times, inmates would get something from their case manager by memo without seeing them. There were times that we were able to do this, but we still needed to see the inmate in person.

Once I started my new system of doing things, I never got behind on my work. I was on top of everything. I would review an inmate file, and adhere to what the judge wanted them to do, along with my recommendation in order for them to complete the job. Wake Correctional Center was basically a work release camp. Most inmates had jobs in the free world.

Once the inmate was two years from being released from prison, I would call them in and make sure they were taking the classes I wanted them to take. The inmates loved my style, because I would go to their dorm to check up on them, and at other times, have a meeting with them on the days I worked late.

I would tell them, "In order for me to help you, you have to help me, help you." I told them in order for them to get what they wanted, they would have to do the things I advised them to do and take the courses I recommended. I told them if they do what I asked, in order to help themselves, I would recommend them for work release or study release, and help them get out on parole. I told the inmates, "If you have five years or more left on your sentence, the only thing I can do is recommend you take certain courses, and stay out of trouble."

The inmates would often say, "Why are you recommending a drug course for me to take when I'm not incarcerated for drugs?"

I told them, "Trust me. I know what I am doing...take every course inside the prison you can take."

What I knew that they didn't know was, when they came up for review, if they had taken a lot of courses, and stayed out of trouble, the chances of them getting work release or getting parole would be greater.

The reason I would give them this advice is because I knew the Parole Board or the Regional Office was not going to give them a thing. If they looked at the inmate record and saw they hadn't been doing anything during their incarceration, they weren't going to get anything.

This is what the inmates didn't know. The Parole Board didn't give damn about what type of courses they were taking. They wanted to see the inmates stay out of trouble, and keep themselves busy by taking those bullshit courses the institution had to offer. That was why I recommended the inmates take drug courses when their crimes were not drug related. I would even have them taking religious courses. The inmates that did what I asked them to do were getting work release, study release, and some were getting parole.

The other inmates that didn't want to do what I asked them to do, saw their fellow inmates getting out of prison and getting the things that they wished they could have. I knew the system like the back of my hand. I knew the Parole Board wanted to see the inmates do something in prison, instead of just doing their time. The inmates didn't know that it was all a game with the Parole Board.

Before long all the inmates on the compound wanted to be on my caseload. The inmates that had five years or more left on their sentence, I would tell them to take their courses. Even though I could recommend them for work, release, study, release, or home leave passes, they weren't going to get it if they didn't work the system (take the courses they offered).

The Work Release Program afforded the inmates the opportunity to get a job in the community while they were still in prison. The Study Release Program was when an inmate was able to enroll in college, and go to college, even while they were still incarcerated. The Home Leave Program (furlough) was when an inmate came close to getting out of prison; they would be able to go home for four hours all the way up to forty-eight hours, then come back to prison. This program was designed to help the inmate re-adjust and re-enter society.

I told them that more than likely they were going to get turned down by parole, even though I'd given my recommendation. I let them know that after they got turned down it was important that they remained out of trouble, and continued taking the courses I recommended. I wanted them to be prepared for this. Most of the time the Parole Board would turn an inmate down even though they knew the inmates were taking courses and staying out of trouble. The Parole Board knew the inmates had a game also.

What the Parole Board wanted to see was if the inmate was sincere about getting out by turning them down, they knew once they turned the inmates down for parole, the inmates were going to stop trying to improve themselves and start back getting in trouble. With this in mind, the next time the inmate came before the Parole Board, they would see that it was all a game, meaning that the inmates were taking those courses to try and fool them.

Once the Parole Board turned them down, the next year they came up for parole. If they were still staying out of trouble, and still trying to improve in areas to better your life, they would say to themselves, 'This person is serious about getting out, because when we turned him down last year, the inmate still stayed out of trouble, and kept taking different courses to better themselves.'

Also, when I was talking to the inmates in the dorm I would tell them, "I don't have a problem seeing you in the office." If they had simple questions like 'when is my release date,' I would tell them to send me a request, and I will more than likely send you a response in the same day."

If I had to set up an appointment to see them, it would take almost a week for me to meet with them. The only thing these inmates wanted to know was, when was their release date or what program I recommended them to take. If they'd sent me a request they would have gotten their answer immediately.

Soon the word got out that I was a 'hands on' case manager, and I didn't have any problems coming on the yard mingling with them. I wasn't afraid of them, and the inmates knew they could talk to me about anything. Some case managers wouldn't even come on the yard and talk with the inmates. It appears that every institution I went to, I was different from everyone else, with my own style.

People fail to realize that once the staff start trying to understand the inmate's request, what they needed, and answer their questions, the inmates wouldn't bother them that much. The job would be much easier.

Of course there were the 'haters.' They would always get jealous because most of the inmates would speak highly of me, and the word would get back to the warden, which made the other staff look bad.

As a matter of fact, when I did something that was working for the benefit of the inmates and the staff, the warden would recommend that the staff follow my lead. He would tell the staff to go on the yard and make themselves visible to the inmates instead of mingling with them on paper. When you adopt my style, the operation of the institution runs smoother.

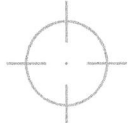

CHAPTER 12

Officer Jackass

There were times when inmates brought in contraband. Yes, they still had their fights and a few more issues, but their aggressions were not taken out on staff.

There was one incident that I remember very well, that happened at Wake Correctional Center. One of the inmates didn't show up for work at his job in the community, (we (staff) didn't take the inmates to work; they would take the city buses to work). We made their schedules, we knew what time their buses reported to their jobs, and we knew what time they had to return to the institution. If an inmate didn't report to work, the employer had to call the institution, and let us know immediately.

One particular day this employer called and told us the inmate walked off the job, but the employer didn't call us right away.

When an inmate doesn't report to work, the institution considers this as an escape. I remember reporting to work at 2:00 p.m. This particular day I noticed when I walked to my office, the staff had a concerned look on their faces. When I got to my office, I asked Martin, "What's going on?"

He said, "An inmate didn't report to work."

I think the inmate was working at a restaurant called Hardees. I went on with my regular routine asking Martin if I could turn the radio station to some R&B. He didn't have a problem with my request, because he'd come to work at 8:00 a.m., and he had been listening to gospel all morning.

My gut instinct told me I was going out to work the escape post. I knew they weren't going to ask Martin, because he was getting off at 4:00 p.m. and they didn't want to pay the overtime. At 3:00 p.m. I received the call from the warden, asking me if I would come to the office.

When I reported to the office, he stated, "I want you to work the escape post. I know you have the experience working as a correctional officer and the fact that you worked at Lorton will make this a piece a cake for you."

"Who is going to be on the post with me?"

I forgot the officer's name but I'm going to name him 'Jackass,' because I saw the way he worked. He treated people like crap. I knew it was going to be a long day and night. This day could have started off great, but Jackass had a tendency to make the lives of people a living hell. He couldn't make my life that way, because I would tell him to get the hell out of my face and that he needed to read my background before he wanted to question me when it came to security.

I remember going to the firearms room, and picking up a Saturday Night Special. My weapon of choice was a .38 caliber; they weren't with the 9 mm back then. I didn't want a shotgun, because I felt like I didn't need one, on top of this, the guy we were looking for, was incarcerated for a misdemeanor crime not a felony.

Officer Jackass was anxious to go capture the inmate, but I wasn't as anxious. I wanted to read everything in the inmate's background before we went out to get him. Checking the background of an inmate is the proper protocol before going after an escapee. I never go on an escape post until I know what I'm dealing with. After reading the inmate's background and discovering that he was locked up on several occasions for trivial crimes, I decided he wasn't going to be a problem.

I knew most inmates that escape always go straight to their comfort zone…home. I don't know why inmates go home when they escape, but they do. Most inmates go out and get them a piece, then turn themselves in, (what I mean by a 'piece' is that they escape and go have sex and get drunk). After they get a piece they feel like they can go back to the prison, and do those other two or three years that they have left of their sentence. Like always, I was in a shirt and tie when I retrieved my weapon; I looked like a detective.

Officer Jackass was the officer who thought he knew everything, and no one else knew anything. He was a typical racist who felt like Blacks didn't know anything. He didn't know that I worked at two institutions, and had a degree in Criminal Justice.

The only way Officer Jackass got the job as an officer was because of politics. We left the institution to go and find the inmate around 4:30 p.m. We had already notified the local police that we had an escaped inmate. As we were departing the institution, I instructed Officer Jackass to drive to the inmate's house. Officer Jackass didn't like taking instructions from a Black man, in particular a smart, Black man.

A mile before we arrived at the inmate's house, I instructed Officer Jackass to slow the vehicle down, and drive about five miles per hour. The inmate knew what the institutional vehicle looked like, and if the inmate was in the house, I didn't want to go all the way to the house to ask his parents if he was in there.

If I had to do that, I would, but if it wasn't necessary I wouldn't. To my surprise he followed my instructions. As we approached the inmate's house, we could see him sitting on the porch with some more guys. I instructed Officer Jackass to park the car, call the institution, and let them be aware that we had spotted the escapee.

The instructions from the institution were to be careful. They would notify the local police to meet us at the house. Officer Jackass couldn't wait for the police; he decided to flood the gas and go one hundred miles per hour to the inmate's house. This officer looked at too much Dukes of Hazard.

As soon as he made the mistake of driving to the inmate's house real fast, the inmate took off running. Officer Jackass and I started running after the inmate Jackass had is weapon drawn. I wasn't planning on using my weapon, unless the inmate stopped running and turned back towards me with something to hurt me. As a matter of fact, it is standard procedure not to shoot anyone when they are running away. When they are running away they are not a threat; they are a threat when they are showing aggression and coming towards you.

In addition to this, this inmate was incarcerated for a probation violation. The fact that I was in shape and could run, I was able to run fast enough to close in on the inmate, that is, until I heard a gun go off. The bullet almost hit me; it landed by my feet. Little did I know that Officer Jackass had fired his weapon!

I stopped when I heard the gun go off. The fact that we were running through the woods, I lost the inmate and didn't know how to get out of the woods. Officer Jackass lived in that neck of the woods, so he knew how to get back to the car. When we got back to the car I radioed the institution and told them, "We chased the inmate through the backwoods of his house, and Officer Jackass fired his weapon."

The warden asked, "Did anyone get hurt?"

"No, but we lost the inmate."

The warden then asked, "Do we need to send the dogs over to your location?"

"Yes," I told him.

When the police arrived with the dogs, we went searching for the inmate. One of the dogs picked up on his scent and went crazy. The dog was worse than Officer Jackass, because the dog had gotten excited about picking up the scent. Nevertheless, we couldn't find the inmate, and what turned into an hour to capture the inmate turned into being in the woods all night until 1:00 a.m.

The warden told us to return to the institution. When we arrived at the institution, I knew we had a load of paperwork to do, because Officer Jackass had fired his weapon, and I wasn't going to tell a lie on the paperwork. When I saw his paperwork it didn't look anywhere near, the report I had written.

Officer Jackass wanted me to justify his firing the weapon. I wasn't going to lie for him. The warden went home; when he came back the next morning, he wanted to know why our reports weren't written alike. I knew he wanted us to get our facts together before we turned in our reports, but I let my report stay as is.

The institution covered for him for firing his weapon (he shouldn't have fired his weapon). A couple of months later my supervisor called me in the office and told me that word came from another institution that I was being transferred. She asked me why I didn't let her know that I had put my paperwork in to go somewhere else.

It wasn't anything personal, but I never let people know when I'm applying for another position or want to leave the institution. My main goal was to get closer to home, get married, and raise my family. I transferred to Goldsboro Correctional Center, which was a few miles from my house. Martin hated to see me leave, but he knew I wanted to get closer to home.

CHAPTER 13

Getting Married, The Hell Begins

Home at last! When I arrived at Goldsboro Correctional Center I was thirty minutes from my hometown. Goldsboro, North Carolina is the home of Seymour Johnson Air Force Base. I finally had a chance to raise my family.

As a matter of fact, before I left Wake Correctional Center, I was engaged to be married on June 2, 1990. As soon as I got to Goldsboro Correctional Center I put in for time off, because my wedding was already scheduled.

My supervisor understood, but he didn't want me to take that much time off from work. I let his thoughts fly over my head, because this was a big day for me. He should have said, 'Go ahead and take the two weeks you had scheduled to take off before you left Wake Correctional Center.'

Nevertheless, the staff wanted me to come in and get straight to work. The institution had been without an extra case manager for quite a while, and two more weeks wasn't going to hurt. Like Wake Correctional Center, they piled my caseload up and gave me the worst inmates, the ones they didn't want to deal with. On June 2, 1990 I finally got married. I awakened that beautiful Saturday morning saying to myself, *this is the day.*

Me And My Grandmother Tessie Jones After My Wedding

Everything was free for me. My barber cut my hair, and my cousin that owned a diner, allowed me to eat a nice breakfast on her. Of course, my best man provided all of the drinks before the wedding. The night before the wedding I stayed at the Sheraton Hotel in Kinston, North Carolina.

I remember going to my hotel room after breakfast without any butterflies in my stomach. I felt fine. The night before, at the rehearsal, with the exception of my brother Terry Jones (Pete), the Coordinator for the wedding smelled alcohol on everyone's breath. She stated, "Please don't come into church tasty for the wedding." I couldn't resist. My brother, Pete, echoed the same thing the coordinator said Saturday afternoon.

He said, "Gold, didn't the lady say don't come into the church tasty?" I looked at Pete and my best man and told him to pour me another shot of Hennessey. Mind you, this was two hours before the wedding. I could tell Pete was mad at me, because I wasn't following orders. Pete said I didn't need to be late for the wedding, and that he was getting ready to go to the church. My brother, is a no nonsense type of guy. He's business minded; I'm the opposite. I told my best man we should finish drinking this bottle of Hennessey before we go to the church. Of course he was down; he didn't mind taking another drink.

After my best man and I finished drinking, he reminded me that we should be heading for the church. On the way to the church, I told him I needed to make a stop. I made my stop and off towards the church we went. When we arrived at the church, I went over to the musician and told him when I walked from the back room with the preacher and my best man,

I wanted him to start off by playing "Joy and Pain" by Frankie Beverly, until we walked in front of the church. I never knew that I would experience more pain than joy after my wedding.

After the marriage ceremony was over, my new bride and I went to the beach later on that night to start our honeymoon. One month later, my wife was pregnant. I couldn't believe she was pregnant! We had already discussed, we weren't going to have any more children until all of our bills were paid.

In my eyes, she became a total stranger to me; her ways were different. In my opinion, she wanted to dominate and know everywhere I went. I didn't have any problems letting her know some things, although I did have a problem with her wanting to know my every move. I tried to deal with what appeared to be mood swings, but I was catching hell. In her eyes I couldn't do anything right. I felt like she wanted me to stop drinking, and just be a henpecked husband.

I never went without paying the bills in the house even when I was drinking. I never allowed alcohol to keep me from paying my bills. Besides I didn't drink everyday, and when I did drink I didn't drink that much. Normally when I drank alcohol, it had a calming effect on me. I never cursed or struck her when I drank. I was just relaxed.

She was a born again Christian, and she conveyed to me on several occasions that she wanted me to give my life to Christ. She knew I wasn't a born again Christian before we got married. When a person is ready to become a born again Christian this decision is left solely between the individual and God. She nagged the hell out me, until I began to not like Jesus.

I had a problem with people invading my space, getting in my face and trying to make me do something. These are not Christ-like ways. I was my own man, and no one could make me do anything except my Grandmother. If she'd lived the Christian life, and let her spiritual light shine, maybe, I would've drawn a lot closer to God. It seemed like when I looked at her I saw satan. To me, she was never satisfied. I can recall telling her that I was going to be a mentor in The Big Brother and Big Sister Program. The only requirement was to spend at least one hour with your mentee, and of course I had to have a background check conducted. I wanted to give back to the community by spending time with a child and being a positive role model. She stated, "You don't even spend time with your own children, and now you want to spend time with someone else's child." I couldn't believe she was saying this. I was planning on bringing the child to the house with my children so that all of us could spend time together. My only regret was allowing her attitude to persuade me to forget the idea.

I recall buying her a car for a surprise. My father had sold it to me for about twelve hundred dollars; the car was pretty decent. I had it parked in the driveway when she got home. She wanted to know whose car it was; I then told her it was her car.

She looked at me as if to say, 'I don't want that crap'; she made it known the next morning. She had a male co-worker pick her up for work. They were friends; he was a paraplegic but had his van customized to accommodate him; she was already about five months pregnant.

It pissed me off for her to have her friend pick her up, not because a male friend came to the house to pick her up for work, but to catch a ride to work after I had just bought her another car was disrespectful. I told her not to bring her behind home after work. I needed time to cool off. When I came home from work she had taken the children, and gone to her mother's house.

The next evening when I came home she had returned, but her mother was at the house. I can't recall how her mother and I got into an argument, but her mother didn't have any problems letting me know that she had a pistol in her pocketbook. I told her mother I could care less about her pistol, because I had been shot before and being shot again wasn't going to change me. Her mother was also a Minister.

I wasn't a violent person; why her mother felt the need to bring a pistol to my house, I will never know. I definitely wasn't going to strike my wife while she was pregnant or any other time. The only time I put my hand on her was when she got in my face, and even then I only moved her to the side to get away from her. She would always get in my face in front of the children; that's what I didn't like.

I knew the game she was playing; it was like, she would start a fight with me in front of the children, and make it seem like I was the troublemaker. I must admit this got on my nerves and I would raise my voice. She would often tell my children I wasn't the man of the house, and that they didn't have to follow my rules, because I was not a Christian.

I was still working with Goldsboro Correctional Center, though later I was hired with the Federal Bureau of Prisons. I remember telling my wife that I had gotten a job as a correctional officer with the Federal Bureau of Prisons. For some reason she didn't like that I had gotten that job. I feel it was because she wanted me to continue to wear a shirt and tie, and carry my briefcase everyday. In my opinion she wanted me to continue to look important, but looking important couldn't pay all the bills. I was hired and my salary went up another ten thousand dollars. I didn't care about going back to wearing uniforms. I felt comfortable either way, whether I was wearing a uniform or suit with a shirt and tie. This really pissed her off. There were a lot of people wearing suits and ties to work that weren't making the money I was making.

I can recall a time when we were getting ready to go to the beach. We had a verbal altercation in the kitchen. I think I recall grabbing her, to move her out the way and when she snatched away from me my hand may have accidentally hit her on the head, but I didn't blatantly hit her intentionally. I was in Law Enforcement; Law Enforcement had zero tolerance for domestic violence. I went into the dining room just to chill out. While there, I remember someone knocking on the door. I went to answer it. It was a man in uniform, a police officer.

He asked, "Are you Garry Jones." "I am."

"Your wife said you hit her and I need to take you down."

"There are two sides to every story and I didn't hit my wife intentionally and she knows it. I grabbed her and moved her out of my way to go into the living room, due to the fact that she was blocking my path. I don't want any trouble considering I am in law enforcement myself."

"Mr. Jones, you are a big guy…will you step outside."

I went outside the house with caution because the policeman's hand was not too far from his weapon. For some reason I felt if I had made the wrong move he was going to shoot.

I asked the policeman, "Take a look at how light my wife's complexion is. If she was any lighter she would be white… look at how petite she is…"

The policeman asked, "What are you trying to tell me?" "If what she is accusing me of is true, I would have left a mark on her and she wouldn't have been able to get up, because if I hit someone they won't be able to move afterwards. Now, who is lying, Mr. Policeman?"

I explained, "I work in Law Enforcement at Goldsboro Correctional Center.

Before the conversation was over, he asked me if I could help him get a job where I worked. ?

Needless to say, we didn't go to the beach that day.

CHAPTER 14

Goldsboro Correctional Center Caseloads

When a new set of inmates arrived at the institution, I would get the bulk of them on my caseload. I knew what they were doing, and I knew it was going to be a matter of time before I spoke up.

I came in on Saturdays to get my caseload together, and to catch my files up. While going through my files, I came across a name from back in the days. The inmate's name was associated with a murder that took place around the corner from my house.

The old lady was raped and murdered; it was in the newspaper. The newspaper said the evidence revealed that the lady was dead before she was raped. How science could figure that out, I don't know; but the guys that were charged, are people I knew very well. I remember when they moved from

Ohio; they were brothers and they never displayed that type of behavior around me.

Anyway, I kept reading Marvin's case file; the more I read the case file the more I knew it was Marvin on my caseload. It wasn't like I didn't remember the name, but I couldn't believe that I would be facing Marvin again, this time on the other side. I would never forget Mrs. Pamela James, the woman who was raped and murdered.

When I paged for Marvin to come to my office, I barely recognized him; he had a beard like Abraham Lincoln and a bald head. Marvin said, "That's Goldwater." I knew he was the right inmate, because he called me by my nickname. I told Marvin to sit down and let me go over some things with him. Marvin had already been locked up for at least fifteen years.

I wanted to ask Marvin if he really raped Mrs. Pamela James, because I did hear that his brother did the raping, but Marvin allegdely took the rap by not snitching on him. I kept it professional by not asking him the question I always wanted to know. Marvin and I talked for a while; I told him what I expected and he understood that I had a job to do.

When I was reading another case file, I recognized a name of someone I didn't know personally, but I'd heard about him when I was a kid. He was involved with supplying North Carolina with drugs, especially heroin. I was about nine years old when he had gotten caught. As a matter of fact, he and another guy were a part of that crew that they made a movie called, American Gangster.

This guy's name was Jorge. He made world news when they had gotten busted. He lived in Goldsboro, N.C., thirty miles from my hometown. When I called him to the office, I went over the things I expected from him and told him I remember hearing about him when I was a kid.

He stated, "I heard you were from Kinston, North Carolina."

"Yes."

"Do you know Sheldon Williams?"

I told him, "Yes, Sheldon is a friend of mine; they called him Shellcat."

He asked me, "Do you know Shellcat's girlfriend?" "Yes, her name is Dedra."

Jorge told me that Dedra was his daughter. "It's a small world."

Sheldon and I grew up right behind one another. We often go to Super Bowls together; to this day, we still travel together once a year. When staff worked at a prison closer to their home, they ran into a lot of people they grew up with, but the inmates from my hometown never expected anything out of me, and they didn't treat me like a homeboy, they treated me with respect. Whenever I would get bored on the job, I would call some homeboys in and talk about old times.

I had some strange times working at Goldsboro Correctional Center. My supervisor would often say, "Mr. Jones, the institution is having an event on this day or that day."

The warden wanted me to come, but if it didn't fit my schedule, I would often say, "No."

"I'll buy you and your wife tickets to attend."

"I have my own money, and if my schedule permits, I'll come."

I found out later, that the warden was putting pressure on my supervisor to make me come to some of the functions at the institution. It wasn't like I wasn't sociable, but I wouldn't let the job interfere with my family life.

There was an incident that happened where my supervisor got in trouble, and I ended up in the middle of it. One day my supervisor called me in the office and said, "Do you have inmate Charles Smith on your caseload?"

"Yes, Charles is quiet and a pretty nice guy, that never gives me any trouble."

My supervisor told me that he wanted me to do the paperwork to get inmate Smith transferred closer to home; I agreed, but there was one thing wrong; inmate Smith hadn't been at the institution long. The proper protocol was to get inmates transferred closer to home, so that it wouldn't be a hardship for the family to visit their loved ones. I liked inmate Smith, but I knew that inmate Smith had gotten an incident report, which is why he was transferred to Goldsboro Correctional Center.

I brought this to the attention of my supervisor (Mr. Henson); that Smith had recently received an incident report, and would have to stay at the institution at least until his six-month review.

Mr. Henson said, and I remember this like it was yesterday, "If you receive any flack (for doing the paperwork), I will take the blame for it."

I did the paperwork against my better judgment, and the warden signed off on it. It bit him in the ass. When inmate Smith's paperwork hit the area office, they looked at his record and realized he had just arrived at Goldsboro Correctional Center with an incident report.

He shouldn't have been recommended for a transfer. I had a reputation of doing my work correctly, and the warden knew I had worked at Triangle Correctional Institution.

As a matter of fact, I called Mr. Combs (the warden), and told him that I wanted to transfer closer to home. He said he knew the warden at Goldsboro Correctional Center. Even though I wasn't working for Mr. Combs anymore, I would still call and ask him for a favor.

Mr. Combs gave Goldsboro Correctional Center a high recommendation on me. The warden at Goldsboro Correctional Institution knew that if Mr. Combs recommended me, that I had to be good, and didn't make many mistakes.

Two days later when I reported to work, I was told to report to the warden's office. When I arrived I saw Mr. Henson, and the assistant warden sitting in the warden's office along with the warden. Mr. Henson looked nervous, and he turned red. Mr. Henson was not a white man, but he was high yellow (real light- skinned). It didn't take a genius to figure out that something was wrong, and my name was written all over it.

Warden Bob asked, "Did you do the paperwork on inmate Smith to be transferred?"

"Yes."

"Who told you to do the paperwork?"

"No one told me to do the paperwork. It's the proper protocol to get an inmate closer to home."

Mr. Bob asked, "Did you get your supervisor's permission to do the paperwork?"

I knew they weren't after me for doing the paperwork on inmate Smith; they were after my supervisor. I was waiting for my supervisor to come to my defense, due to the fact that he was the one that told me to do the paperwork. He just sat in his chair and didn't say a word.

I said to myself, 'This man is getting ready to let me take the fall for some crap he told me to do.' The warden asked me again, "Did your supervisor know you were doing the paperwork?"

I stood in silence waiting for my supervisor to get me out of his bullshit that he'd gotten me caught up in, but he refused to do so. The warden already had my supervisor, because he signed off on the paperwork; he just wanted me to confirm what he already knew. The warden asked me again in a loud tone…

"Did Mr. Henson tell you to do this paperwork!" I told him in a loud tone, "No, he did not!"

The warden got mad and said, "I should fire you right now, but I'm going to give you one more chance." This time the warden raised his voice and stuck his finger in my face and said, "Did Mr. Henson tell you to do the paperwork!"

I slapped the warden's finger out of my face and told him, "Don't ever put your finger in my face or yell at me again!"

Assistant Warden Edwards came over and acted like he wanted to grab me. I told him he better not touch me. Mr. Edwards told me to leave the office. When I walked out of the warden's office I knew I had lost my job, but then I thought about it; he put his finger in my face. If I'm out of a job, so is he, because a warden should never raise his voice at a staff member or put his finger in a staff member's face.

I walked back to my office pissed off at my supervisor, because he betrayed me. He came to my office and said, "Mr. Jones can I talk to you?"

"Yes."

"I know you must think I'm no good for not saying anything, and not coming to your defense."

"What you are saying is an understatement. You let me take a fall for something you told me to do."

Mr. Henson said, "Yes, you are right Mr. Jones, but I have twenty-eight years of service with the government and I have two more years to retire. Mr. Jones you are a young man with a bright future ahead of you"…

As I was listening to him, I couldn't believe what I was hearing.

"I just slapped the warden's finger out of my face, and I have a bright future ahead of me? What kind of crap is this Mr. Henson? I'm getting ready to lose my job and I just got married."

Mr. Henson said, "I doubt if you lose your job Mr. Jones. The warden was out of line for putting his finger in your face. He wouldn't dare take a chance on firing you. He has more to lose than you do."

I looked at Mr. Henson and said, "Man, I don't have any respect for you anymore, because you let me take a fall to save your own career."

After this incident, I knew this was not the place I wanted to be. I put in my paperwork to work at the Federal Prison Camp at Seymour Johnson Air Force Base. Three months later, I got a call from my supervisor to come to his office. When I reported to the supervisor's office, he told me the institution was having a banquet. He wanted my wife and I to attend, and he would buy the tickets. I told him, "I am not interested in attending the function," and walked out of the office.

Two hours later, the supervisor came to my office and said that the warden wanted me to come by the office. I went to the warden's office and he said, "I heard you don't want to attend the banquet. I have in my hand an evaluation that the Federal Prison Camp wants me to sign, and one of the questions they are asking, is, 'Are you a team player?' I can determine whether you get this job that you want, with a stroke of a pen."

"I don't care what you put on the paperwork. I'm not attending the banquet. Ever since I came to your institution, I felt like I wasn't welcome. Your staff is envious of me, because they lack the courage to stand up for themselves, the way I do."

He said, "Mr. Jones you are very smart and courageous, and I think you will have a great career with the Bureau of Prisons; but before you leave this institution I just want you to attend the banquet, because most of the black staff don't attend the functions we have at the institution."

"I understand why they don't attend, considering the way they are treated around here."

The warden broke down and apologized to me for putting his finger in my face. In my heart I knew he was going to sign off on my paperwork for me to go work with the Federal Bureau of Prisons. After consideration, I thought to myself, that if he was man enough to apologize, then I was man enough to give in and attend the banquet. One month later I was hired by the FBOP.

CHAPTER 15

Federal Prison Camp Seymour Johnson

Jones is Correctional Officer of Year

January 26, 1991 was the day after my twenty-seventh birthday; I'd finally started my career with the Federal

Bureau of Prisons. My first stop was the Federal Prison Camp at Seymour Johnson Air Force Base, the home of the F-15 fighter jets; the first jets that struck serious blows in the first Gulf War.

Even though Seymour Johnson was an Air Force base, a Federal Prison was built there. Inmates worked on the base, which would eventually cause the Air Force to offer some of the airmen an early retirement after only fifteen years of service.

Inmates worked everywhere the airmen worked, and they did everything the airmen would do, such as cleaning, landscaping duties, NCO (Non Commission Officer) club; some of the inmates were assigned to work at the site where the F-15's were located. A lot of people don't realize, when inmates start working on base, the civilians lose their jobs, due to the fact, the government pays inmates slave labor compared to paying civilians minimum wages or more. In addition to this the government has to pay for the health care of civilians, whereas, with inmates, they don't.

I noticed at every prison I worked they followed the same trend…inmates make the same products the 'free world' was making. The companies that subcontracted their products to the government, become filthy rich. They knew they could get their products made in prison, for much of nothing, and not have to go through the middleman. They bought directly from the government, and to this day they still do.

Inmates make products for car dealerships, work for major airlines and computer companies; inmates do the work for travel agents; they make sensors that go on missiles. Now I understand why when we go to war, the bombs don't hit their targets, because if someone pissed an inmate off that particular day, the inmate could screw up something.

Of course the government has inspections, but they can't inspect every sensor that is made. Phone companies are laying off civilians and using inmate services, but the government will tell people that their job is moving overseas, when in reality their job is moving into a prison for the inmates to do. The next time you call 411, and the person on the other end of the line says, "City and state, please," don't be surprised if you are talking with an inmate.

This country was built off slave labor and we continue to use slave labor inside the prisons, if not inside the prison; the jobs are outsourced to other countries for slave labor or to illegal immigrants coming across the borders. The government tells us that the inmates need to do something with their time, and they are learning a skill, but when they are released from prison, how can they utilize their skills if they are competing with their fellow inmates and other civilians to get a job?

If they are not competing with their fellow inmates or other civilians, they are not getting hired at all, because most companies ask, 'Have you ever been convicted of a crime.' If the inmates write 'no' on their application, and the company finds out later on that they lied…they'll get fired. If they put 'yes,' most of the time they won't get hired. I'm not sharing with you what I heard, I'm sharing with you what I know, what I've seen and what I've experienced working inside prisons.

Do you remember the commercial that came out about prison blues; this was a clothing item. In the commercial, they said, 'The product was made on the inside and worn on the outside.' What they were telling you, is the clothing items were made inside the prison, and the people on the outside wore them.

The U.S. citizens never understood what the commercial was talking about. When you buy your products straight from the prison, you don't have to worry about the union or paying your employees minimum wages. This is why lobbyists and large companies donate to politicians, because they can get them to make up strict laws to insure the inmates stay in prison forever for committing a non-violent crime.

The reason lobbyists and large companies lobby for the strict laws to either send people to prison or the people who are in prison to never see the streets again, is because they want the inmates to continue to make their products. Working at the Federal Prison Camp Seymour Johnson Air Force base wasn't any different.

When I was hired at this prison, I had to take an I.F. class called Institution Familiarization. This class talked about the operation of the institution. The class talked about ethics, conduct, not getting in debt, and how to keep your credit score up. The reason they were teaching all of this information was because the inmates knew how to use staff's personal information against them. If a staff member were weak, they would fall for it.

If staff were in debt, that meant they were vulnerable to the lure of making money inside the prison. Knowing the staff was in debt was a motivator for the inmate to pursue staff to bring contraband inside the prison. Bringing in contraband was a quick way of making big money.

When the instructor brought up people having bad credit, I told the instructor I had bad credit. The instructor told me that no one in the classroom had bad credit or they wouldn't have hired him or her.

I told the instructor the bureau must have skipped over my credit report. I knew I had bad credit, due to fifteen thousand dollars worth of hospital bills from when I was shot in a club while in college and due to the fact that my roommates didn't pay my rent when I was in the hospital.

The instructor told me again that my credit was good. For some strange reason I knew this credit report was going to come back and haunt me; I told the instructor the truth. My wife was pregnant with my youngest son and I didn't want to lose my job over bullshit, mind you this was on January 28, 1991.

My class went through this training for a week. The next week, which was February we went to Glynco, Georgia for the Bureau of Prisons training. The training entailed how to find contraband, how to shoot a weapon, what to do if we were held hostage, and some more important things we needed to know about working in a prison.

I went through that training without studying that much, because most of the information was easy to me, because I had worked at four institutions prior to being hired with the Bureau of Prisons. Of course every training session I attended, there was some kind of excitement once class was over.

Friday nights we would go out to this famous place that I think was called, 'Pier 1.' Don't quote me on the name, because it has been a long time since I've been to Glynco, Georgia.

In my opinion Glynco, Georgia was a redneck town. Most of their revenues came from the Bureau of Prisons, because Glynco has a big training center for the Bureau of Prisons, as well as other federal agencies.

I remember one night we went out to this club. One of my buddies was sitting with this honey he had met, as a matter of fact I was sitting at the table as well. This lady came over to the table and hit this honey upside the head with a bottle; obviously she wanted to be with my partner also.

When the ladies started to fight, I told my partner, "Let's go!"

As we were leaving the club my partner said, "Man, I need to go back in there and get the lady's phone number." "No, let's go back to the training facility!"

Anyway the fight came to the outside of the club, and one guy picked up a bottle and shouted, "That is the guy she was sitting with!" I told my partner, "We have to go, we are not white; we can't afford to get caught up in nothing."

I was so glad the police drove up that I didn't know what to do. We made it back to the training facility safely, and the incident was never brought up again. When we returned to our assigned institution, it was business as usual for me. I did my job the way it was supposed to be done.

As a matter of fact, I left the Glynco training facility early Saturday morning and the next afternoon, my son was born. He was named after Malcolm X; I was reading The Autobiography of Malcolm X prior to his birth, which is how I came up with his name.

Shortly after I came back from Glynco, Georgia training facility, the Office of Internal Affairs came to the institution to visit me about my background check.

The very thing I thought would come back to haunt me had arrived…my credit report, that I mentioned to the instructor.

My credit was bad, and they had to recommend that I get dismissed from the Bureau of Prisons. They stated I should have told them about my credit. I explained to the investigator that I told the instructor about my credit and that my instructor stated, "I didn't have bad credit or I wouldn't be sitting in the classroom."

When the investigator went to talk with the I.F. instructor, he lied and said I didn't mention anything about my credit.

Since the instructor decided to lie, I gathered up everyone that was in my class, and asked them to write a memo of what I told the instructor about my credit. To my amazement, my class remembered me telling the instructor this information. They all wrote a memo on my behalf, stating that I did pose this question in I.F. training.

The instructor that was the training coordinator tried to cover his backside, because he knew he hadn't run a credit check on me. When I pulled up my credit report, I saw where the federal government made an inquiry in the middle of February, when they were supposed to run your credit before they hired you.

I talked with the warden and he said I would not get fired, because of the memos my classmates wrote the Internal Affairs agent. I was forthright. The warden told me that I needed to make payments on the hospital bills and turn them in personally.

I called my lawyer, who wrote a letter to the warden explaining to him that I had been trying to get my credit straightened out before I started working with the bureau. My attorney explained to him that I had gotten shot, and when we went to sue the establishment the club had liquidated their assets. Therefore, they didn't have any money to pay for my doctor bills.

I had veterans insurance from my stepfather, but my hometown hospital, Lenoir County Hospital, wanted me to pay the hospital bills, and let my insurance pay me back. I didn't have this type of money. My hospital bills from Duke Hospital were paid, because they filed my VA insurance and got every penny that was owed to them.

Lenoir County Hospital would have gotten their money if they had filed my VA Insurance, but they wanted to play hardball and they didn't get anything. I called my stepfather Nick who was in Texas and explained what happened.

He said he would contact the VA, and ask them to get involved. The VA stated if the hospital would file the insurance, they would pay the bill. After all those years (five), Lenoir County Hospital finally filed the insurance, and they received their money. It took the Bureau of Prison one year to give me clearance.

Normally, the institution will give clearance within three months. I'm glad the bureau didn't check my credit report, because I wouldn't be here writing about how crooked their system is. To me it was a blessing in disguise.

CHAPTER 16

My First House

In September 1993, my family and I moved into our first house. No more renting. It was great, because my electric bill was only seventy-five dollars a month compared to four hundred dollars per month in the house that I was renting. I think my mortgage payment was five hundred seventy-five dollars per month, compared to the four hundred dollars per month I was paying for rent. I would've been in a house prior to this if my credit wasn't bad.

There was this woman that helped me get my credit straight. She wanted to sell a house so badly, that she helped me get my credit straight. When I got my credit halfway straight, she said she could get me in the house whenever I wanted to move.

With my income, it would be easy for me to get in the house. I went home and explained this to my wife, who was pissed, because for some reason she thought her name wasn't going to be put on the house. In my opinion, she was insecure about this and other things. She told me that she didn't like the idea. I had to go back and explain to the lady that my wife said, 'No,' about the idea she suggested.

Needless to say, my wife had to work on her credit. It took us about another year to even get the house. She was working with the city of Kinston, and applied for a job at an elementary school. Being that she had very good clerical skills, she was hired for the job.

This brought in more income; our chances of owning our first home was getting closer, because she was making more money. The house we moved into was a new house. I don't think my wife was pleased with the house , because the house wasn't all brick. I explained to her that this was a 'starter' home for us and when we started making more money in the future she could get that all brick home. I explained to her, we couldn't afford some of the houses that had brick facing around them.

I think most women would have been thrilled about having a new home, but my wife's demeanor indicated to me she was not a happier camper. It had gotten to the point that I was beginning to have anxiety attacks staying with this woman. Everything had to be her way. She wasn't satisfied with the car or the new house. I feel she didn't care for my friends, especially the ones that weren't married. I couldn't leave the house without her complaining over trivial matters. She would often get mad at me, because my relatives would buy things for the children. I told her I couldn't help it if my relatives loved buying things for their great nephews and great niece.

She would always say, "Your family is not going to let you be a man and buy things for your children." I bought a lot of things for my children; I supplied my children with everything they needed, and when my aunts and uncle bought things for them, this was even better for the kids. I didn't hear the kids complaining; they loved it! She was determined that she was going to take me through hell until I humbled myself to her. I give respect when respect is due, and if I don't get respect from a person, then it's hard for me to continue to give them respect.

My wife would talk about my family in disrespectful ways, even though I would get mad, she would continue to talk about them. My family always treated her with the utmost respect, but they didn't have any idea that she had spoken so terribly about them. She knew I loved my uncle, but she would talk about him in a very negative way, even after she began working at the school where he was a principal. She would often come home and say he spoke in a disrespectful manner to the teachers.

I knew my uncle; he would often joke with his teachers. My wife also knew that he loved to joke. I must admit there were times when he had to put teachers in their place, especially when their classrooms would get out of hand. I knew my uncle would never disrespect anyone. Even though I knew this was not true, I still got mad when she would lie on him.

She didn't say too much about my grandmother, but she used to say, "When you get married you are supposed to leave your parents and cling to each other," (leaving everyone else behind).

She told me, I shouldn't have a key to my grandmother's house. This was a family house and each of the grandchildren had keys to the house. I still have keys today. I would often go to my grandmother's house when I wanted a good meal and my clothes ironed. My wife wouldn't iron my uniforms, but my grandmother didn't have any problems ironing and washing my clothes. Why should I take my uniforms to the cleaners when I could pay my grandmother to wash and press them? My grandmother was a great cook, great ironer and seamstress.

My wife would often go to church, shout, come home and raise all kinds of hell. No one is perfect and it's impossible to live a perfect life. I too, have my faults, but I don't play with God. She had good ways also. She kept an immaculate house and for the most part was a good mother to the children, (outside of making our daughter feel bad (insecure). My wife was never filthy and she didn't walk out of the house looking thrown away. She took pride in herself, but she made sure she made my life a living hell.

My oldest son was very intelligent and he applied himself very well in school. I was not his biological father, but I had been a father to him since he was three years old.

My daughter was a C-student, but could have been an A or B student if she would have applied herself. My wife would make comments about her being an underachiever, just to make me mad, but my daughter was also her daughter. The reason my daughter was treated differently was because she had my ways and looked like me. I refused to let my wife make her feel less important than her oldest brother. I loved them both, but I could tell my daughter's self-esteem was low because of some of the things her mother would say to her.

My baby son was too young, so it didn't matter what was going on around the house with him. My daughter was a very sick child just like I was when I was growing up and my youngest child used to get sick a lot also.

Earlier, in my marriage my wife made the statement, "You don't do anything but 'produce sick children.'" This was a horrible thing to say. The reason she made this statement was because my daughter was very sick at an early age. She suffered from asthma just as I did, when I was growing up.

When my daughter was younger, she always had ear infections; we were always taking her to the doctor, almost every two weeks. Then my daughter started catching pneumonia. Later on the doctors found out why she was contracting infections that were leading to pneumonia. They informed us that her patent ductus arteriosus (PDA) didn't close after birth.

At eighteen months my daughter had to have surgery to correct the problem. This type of surgery is performed by a cardiothoracic (treatment of the heart), and requires general anesthesia. The surgery required a small incision in the left side of the chest. After the surgery was done, my daughter stayed in the hospital for about a week. After the surgery she didn't have any more problems with infections or pneumonia, but the doctor stated after the surgery that my daughter had entirely too much blood in her urine and we needed to keep a check on her by taking her to the doctor.

After taking my daughter back and forth to the doctor for blood in the urine, she eventually had to go see a nephrologist (kidney specialist). They did every test they could do to find out where the blood was coming from. Eventually the doctors needed to explore more, and had to give her a kidney biopsy.

My wife stated, "I am not going to allow the doctors to give her a kidney biopsy!"

That was when I really got angry...my daughter's life was at stake!

Every specialist we visited performed the same test and recommended my daughter have a kidney biopsy to find out exactly what was going on. Since my wife was non-receptive for what the doctors wanted to do, they informed us that my daughter needed to see a kidney specialist every six months, to keep a close eye on what was going. My wife and I argued over this for years.

She always said, "Let the Lord handle it."

I'm a strong believer of the miracles the Lord can perform, but he didn't put doctors on this earth for nothing. Miracles are performed everyday through the doctors, from the Lord.

I wanted to have the procedure done, but she refused to do this, until we moved to Tallahassee. After going back and forth for almost twelve years, my wife finally decided to allow the doctors to perform the kidney biopsy on my daughter.

The procedure didn't take long. My daughter only stayed in the hospital for about three days. With the kidney biopsy being performed the doctors found out more about my daughter's condition. As for asthma, my daughter eventually grew out of it.

When my youngest child was born, he was healthy until he started developing high fevers, which caused him to start having seizures. The doctor stated this was normal for some children to have seizures when they contract an infection and fevers. My son was put in the hospital to have fluid drawn from his spinal cord to ensure he didn't have meningitis, the test showed negative.

The doctors stated, "If you can control his fever, he won't have seizures anymore."

Needless to say, my son is quite healthy now.

At one point in our marriage, (in 1996), I asked my wife to have another baby. She refused to have another child, again stating, "You produce sick children."

When my wife would say I produced nothing but sick kids, this would bother me, because she birthed all three children. In my mind I asked myself, was I sleeping with the enemy?. I continued to go to work, come home and be miserable.

She would always complain that I wasn't a family man, but I beg to differ. I always spent time with my family. We went to the beach during the summer almost every week. If the children didn't catch the bus, I would take them to school and pick them up faithfully. I usually cooked for them before my wife would get off from work, because I usually worked the swing shift, which meant I was home during this time. Every chance we got, I would take them to amusement parks such as King's Dominion on the outskirts of Richmond Virginia, Six Flags over Georgia in Atlanta, Walt Disney World in Orlando, Florida and to the fair every year.

If I never go to another amusement park again, I won't be disappointed. As a matter of fact when amusement parks are mentioned around me I have a panic attack. I worked it into my schedule to attend all of the children's school functions and activities.

I used to go to my children's schools and surprise them. I would sit and eat lunch with them. On my days off, I would meet my wife for lunch. We would take the children to the movies and have birthday parties for them. I did everything a husband or a family man was required to do. Yet, my wife would still find something to complain or nag about.

As long as I was home, she was satisfied. Although, sometimes when I was there she still complained about one thing or another. I almost literally lost my mind, but I hung in the marriage even when I wasn't happy. I think I did this because of the kids.

Surprise Visit At My Youngest Son's School

CHAPTER 17

Special Investigative Supervisor

Working at Federal Prison Camp Seymour Johnson was a piece of cake for me, because I knew the prison system like the back of my hand. When the lieutenants found out I worked at Lorton (which is tougher than the hard core state prisons), they knew I didn't need a lot of supervision.

They all said if I worked at Lorton, I could work anywhere in the world. They didn't have to worry about supervising me; I was well trained and groomed in this area. I enjoyed working for certain lieutenants, because they were down to earth.

I also worked for a redneck captain. He left two months after I arrived, but that redneck never gave me any trouble. I never understood why, but he was very cordial with me.

After the captain left, Captain Ramos was hired; I liked working for him too. He was cool. He always came to work dressed like someone from Miami Vice.

After the other lieutenant's left, there weren't too many other lieutenants I enjoyed working for. As a matter of fact, shortly after they left I became a lieutenant myself; they would always call to check on me, even though they were working at other institutions. After Captain Ramos left, he would call and check on me as well.

I remember working with another captain. I used to get mad at him, because he would let other departments run over correctional services. He was always bragging about how he worked the S.I.S (Special Investigative Supervisor). position for ten years, but when I became a

S.I.S. lieutenant he couldn't teach me a thing. Every time I went to him for help he couldn't give me any advice. When I was a regular lieutenant, he would always throw his work off on me. I hated when he asked me to do something, because he never knew what he wanted done.

This used to frustrate me, because, 'How can you tell me to do something when you don't know what you want done?' He couldn't explain anything to me. It took me forever to figure out what he wanted done.

I can't stand working for people who don't know what they want done.

I remember going to F.C.I. Butner to get some 'hands on' training for the S.I.S. (Special Investigative Supervisor) position. I went there for a week to get this training.

Within that week, the Federal Building in Oklahoma got blown up. The director of the Federal Bureau of Prisons instructed everyone to return to his or her respective institutions; my training was cut short.

I had been in Colorado for Special Investigative Supervisor training, but I needed more training in a real institution. When I returned to Seymour Johnson, the S.I.S. lieutenant was instructed to lock up all the Nation of Islam inmates. Someone called in and said, 'The Nation of Islam was responsible for the blowing up of the Federal Building in Oklahoma.'

I told the captain, "We can't put all of the Nation of Islam inmates in the hole or Special Housing Unit; we only have ten cells. The rest of the inmates would have to be transferred to the county jail..."

"If we lock up the Nation of Islam and we don't have concrete information that they had anything to do with the Oklahoma bombing, we are going to have a serious riot on our hands!"

The captain said, "Jones, these are not my instructions; these instructions are coming from the director of the Federal Bureau of Prisons."

"Someone needs to tell the warden this is not a good idea! He needs to call the director and let her know this is not a good idea!"

We needed more information before we started locking people up.

Needless to say, after it was all over with, the Nation of Islam didn't have a damn thing to do with the bombing in Oklahoma. Some guy named Timothy McVeigh orchestrated the whole thing with all of his militia groups that hated the government.

I received word from another inmate that this white inmate had a lot of articles on militia groups, as well as Timothy

McVeigh. I went to search the inmate's locker, turns out, the snitch was telling the truth about this inmate. I did the investigation and had him transferred to another prison. The Bureau of Prisons should have known that black people don't blow up a damn thing; they may riot in the streets but they aren't blowing up anything.

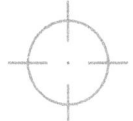

CHAPTER 18

F.C.I. Tallahassee, Tallahassee Florida

After I made the decision to move to Tallahassee, my mind and soul began to go on an emotional roller coaster. Again, I was faced with stepping out of my comfort zone, and moving to another state, only this time I was taking my family with me. I would question myself everyday on whether or not I made the right decision. How would my decision affect my children?

My oldest son was in the tenth grade, and my daughter was in the seventh grade. My wife was excited about moving to Florida, but I knew when you have a child that is in the tenth grade it could destroy their self-esteem. They have their friends, and don't want to leave them behind to go to a place where they don't have any friends or relatives.

I was definitely apprehensive, because my future supervisor wasn't accepting me.

I remember when I first received the announcement that I was getting promoted and going to Tallahassee.

The former warden from Federal Prison Camp at Seymour Johnson was now the warden at the Federal Correctional Institution at Tallahassee. He came to town because he still had some personal items in storage that he needed to pick up. Normally when a person gets promoted in the bureau, the captain calls him or her in the office to let them know they've been promoted; then the person decides when they want to start their new position. My promotion didn't take place like the status quo.

The warden came to the institution (Seymour Johnson), while I was working and said, "Congratulations Lieutenant Jones, I have selected you to be one of my GS-11 lieutenants (senior lieutenant). I'm looking forward to seeing you in Tallahassee." He said he was back in North Carolina on business, and decided to tell me in person that I was going to Tallahassee.

Staff on the compound was making up rumors that the warden left Tallahassee just to come and tell me that I was being promoted. Of course people were saying, "He is the warden's boy," but they couldn't be further from the truth. They didn't know this warden. He was strictly by the book and he knew that I was a stern, yet fair lieutenant that would get the job done.

I was apprehensive about going to Tallahassee because I'd I heard so much about going into a redneck country, and my future supervisor (the captain) didn't make it easy for me. After I got selected to go to Tallahassee, I called the captain to thank him for allowing me to be one of his lieutenants. He never returned my phone call. I emailed the captain and thanked him, but he never returned my email.

It didn't take a genius to figure out the captain, didn't like me, even though he didn't know me. I remember emailing the captain to let him know my wife and I would be coming to Tallahassee for a house-hunting trip, and I wanted to come by the institution to visit.

Again, the captain didn't return my email. You could only imagine

Presented with One of Many Awards

how I felt, leaving my comfort zone and going to work for a supervisor who didn't accept me. Even though I was a warrior, when my plane touched down in Tallahassee, Florida, I had butterflies in my stomach.

My wife and son didn't know how I was feeling, but I knew I was in for a war. We checked into the hotel, and the next day I went to visit the institution. I stopped by the warden's office; he took me straight to the lieutenant's office and introduced me to the other lieutenants. I remember the warden saying, "This is Lieutenant Jones, he will be a new lieutenant here at Tallahassee. I want you all to show him around the institution."

There were four lieutenants in the office, three whites and one black. None of the white lieutenants shook my hand, nor did they say anything. I remember the black lieutenant, whose name was Lieutenant Caldwell, came over to shake my hand, and said, "I'll show you around."

Lieutenant Caldwell and I would become the very best of friends. Little did I know that Lieutenant Caldwell was experiencing racism at F.C.I. Tallahassee...I would become their next victim.

When he walked around the compound, introducing me to other staff members, he asked, "Do you know what you are up against?"

"Yes," I told the lieutenant, "I knew what I was up against before I left North Carolina."

Lieutenant Caldwell and I made it to the dining hall – another reference used other than mainline - to finish meeting the rest of the staff. Before Caldwell could get it out of his mouth, I interrupted him and said, "The white man with the suit and tie is the captain."

"How do you know?"

"I could feel my stomach turning on the inside when I saw him."

Lieutenant Caldwell introduced me to the captain. "You are Lieutenant Jones."

"Yes."

The captain stuck his hand out for me to shake; I wouldn't shake it; he knew why. The captain knew that I was aware of the fact that he didn't want me at Tallahassee. Even though I didn't ask the captain anything, he proceeded to explain to me why he didn't respond or call me back. I knew right then he felt guilty. I knew I couldn't trust him at all.

The captain is the lieutenant's supervisor and if you have someone working under you, it's your job to make sure the person under you has the tools that are needed to operate. I was a lieutenant under this captain. Later on, after my tour, I went back to the hotel with my wife and son, and told them we needed to start looking for a house to live in.

Needless to say, we couldn't find a house suitable for her so therefore, we applied to live in staff housing. Staff housing is located on the grounds of the institution. During that time, most of the people living in staff housing included the warden, supervisor, lieutenant or a department head.

When we left to return to North Carolina, I said to myself, 'I will be very prepared to fight any battle I have to.' I equipped myself with the breastplate of knowledge, the heart of David, and the leadership of Moses.

CHAPTER 19

The Boys in Blue Again

When I arrived in Tallahassee in July 1995, the house at the institution was not ready for me and my family to move into. We had to stay in the hotel for about five weeks. Of course the government was paying for everything. I had to make sure I kept receipts for everything we purchased. I definitely didn't want to be charged with misappropriation of government funds or trying to defraud the government. Like I said earlier, I wasn't well received by my captain, and I wanted to make sure I didn't give them any ammunition to fire me.

It was a Saturday evening when I got off work. When I got back to the hotel, my family wasn't there so I took a nap. When the family returned to the hotel, my wife had some shopping bags. She said she took the kids to the library and downtown Tallahassee while I was at work. I remember asking her if she spent any money from the government allowance. We were able to spend some money, but I wanted to make sure if we did go over the amount, we had enough to cover the expenses. She never answered my question; she just ignored me. I asked her again. Again she didn't answer. I wanted to see the receipts, but she refused to let me see them. She said they were in her purse. After arguing with her about the receipts, I grabbed her purse to get the receipts; she snatched it away from me. I told her I needed those receipts. I grabbed her purse again to get the receipts, but she grabbed the purse away from me again. I turned around and I could see the kids looking at us so I decided to leave it alone. When I was walking to my room (we had a two bedroom suite), a drinking glass came across the room passed my head and hit the wall. I said to myself, 'I know this lady didn't throw a glass at me.' I ignored what she'd done and proceeded into the bedroom and locked the door. I was pissed, because she was starting trouble again in front of the kids and making me look like the bad guy.

After I got into my room, I called my daughter from the hotel room to the main room. Of course I could've walked back in the room where my wife was located, but I didn't need the trouble. I asked my son and daughter if they wanted me to order a pizza for them and they said, 'Yes.' I turned on the TV and started watching the O.J. Simpson trial clipping for the week, while waiting for the pizza to be delivered. Ten minutes later I received a hard knock on my hotel door. I jumped up and said to myself, 'Who is knocking on my room door this hard; surely it couldn't be the pizza delivery man.' I went to the door and before I could answer it, the knock got louder with force this time as if someone was trying to break in the room. I didn't know anyone in Tallahassee. 'Certainly no one could have been looking for me. Perhaps it is someone with the wrong room,' I thought.

As I was grabbing the door handle to open the door, the police burst into the room and asked, "Are you Garry Jones?"

"I am."

The police officer was reaching for his gun.

"You better use it, because I am not going down without a fight! What do you want?"

"We received a call that you assaulted your wife."

This had to be a mistake, because she was in the other room, nowhere near me.

"Your wife said you assaulted her…I need to take you in."

"I am not going anywhere, because I didn't assault her."

During that time the police were locking up all men that had been accused of assault, because it was during the time O.J. Simpson was accused of assaulting and killing his wife. The police didn't want to hear anything I had to say. During that time the only thing a woman had to do is call the police and say a man hit her; they would take the woman's word one hundred percent of the time. The O.J. The Simpson trial made it hard for a black man.

I proceeded to tell the police, "I am a lieutenant with the Federal Bureau of Prisons and domestic violence isn't tolerated…I didn't hit her."

"We just moved to Tallahassee; today was my first day at work."

The police weren't trying to hear a thing I had to say. The only thing going through my mind was, 'I'm getting ready to get fired over a damn lie. Every time this lady gets mad at me she will call the police stating that I hit her.' I had come to the conclusion that she would do anything to get me fired when she got mad.

The sad thing about the whole situation was that if I lost my job, I wouldn't be able to support my family especially if I had an assault charge, which meant I would not be able to support her and the children. She should have thought of this fact.

A few minutes later, a female police officer came out of the other room where my children were. I was surprised, because I wanted to know where she came from. I didn't know that one policeman came to my room and the female police officer went to the other room. Like I said earlier my family and I had a two- bedroom suite.

After the female police officer interviewed the children, they said I didn't hit her. Of course they didn't ask my youngest anything, because he was about four years old. My two oldest children told the police that my wife and I were arguing, and after the argument I left to go to my room; they told the officer she had thrown a glass at me and that I went into the other bedroom and locked it so she couldn't come in.

The male police officer said, "If I receive another call from your wife, I am going to take you down and lock you up."

I looked at him and said to myself this man just heard my children say, I didn't hit her, but he was planning on locking me up if he had to come back.

A few minutes later the pizza man came with the pizza, and I called my children to come to my room to get their pizza. The only thing I could think about was what that policeman said to me. I thought to myself, 'The only thing she has to do is lie and I'm going to jail.' I sat in silence for a couple of hours trying to figure out what I was going to do. After thinking for a couple of hours I made my mind up. I would send my wife and children back to North Carolina. I didn't need the headache.

I called my oldest son into my room and we went to the bank across the street. I withdrew some money from the ATM and gave it to him. I told him I was sending them back to North Carolina, and was letting them take one of the cars back. The money I gave him was enough money to go back to North Carolina. I told him I would get their things out of storage, and send it to them. When my son and I got back to the room he gave the money to my wife. I told her she needed to leave, because I wasn't going to start a new career with her calling the police whenever she got mad.

The next day came; I didn't hear any movement in the room. I went inside to see if the children and my wife got their things together to get ready to move, but they were still asleep. My wife refused to move back to North Carolina. I guess she was too embarrassed to have to move back to North Carolina, after having been in Florida for just a few days. The people back home would've been trying to figure out what happened considering we had a big, send off party.

Needless to say, my wife and the family never moved back so I dealt with her crap, because I wanted to keep the marriage for the kids.

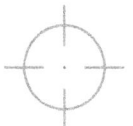

CHAPTER 20

The First Working Day at F.C.I. Tallahassee

On July 12, 1995, I reported to Tallahassee for work. I knew my job very well, but I had to learn the layout of the institution. The captain called me into his office, and said the Special Operations Response Team (S.O.R.T.) the lieutenant was stepping down and he needed me to fill that position.

The S.O.R.T lieutenant is in charge of training officers on how to go to combat, whether it's fighting in a riot, conducting forced cell movements or anything that had to do with emergencies. I didn't want the position, but everyone else would have died to get the position.

I guess the captain looked at me as if I was a pretty big guy, so therefore, I could handle the job. He really didn't want me in this position, but in order to be a S.O.R.T. lieutenant, we had to be a GS-11 senior lieutenant. The captain wanted 'his boy' in the position, but he was just an activities lieutenant and the captain put him under me.

On the real side, I wasn't up for the position, mentally or physically. Physically, I always trained as a weightlifter, and mentally I didn't care anything about shooting, cleaning weapons, jumping and climbing walls, and running five miles in uniform. I was never in the military; I knew I wasn't cut out to be in this prestige position.

Coming Down the Wall at S.O.R.T. Training

I had a meeting with the activities lieutenant. I told him he could train the officers on how to be on the S.O.R.T. team, but I also advised him that nothing goes on without me knowing about it. The activities lieutenant was very cocky and the captain loved him. Needless to say he didn't like me being in charge over him.

Training

The lieutenant would try to undermine me whenever he had the chance. The fact of the matter is he didn't want to follow orders coming from a black lieutenant, even though I told him he could run the show. He would often call meetings with the team without my awareness; at these times the captain would look at me when I came to work as if to say, 'Why are you in the institution when you're supposed to be in training?'

The captain knew what was going on, because he set this up with him to undermine me. I took the high road since I was the senior lieutenant; I called a meeting with the activities lieutenant and informed him that we needed to get on the right page.

We need to try to get along in front of the other members of the team, but if we needed to air some things out, we could always take our differences to the parking lot. I also informed him to stop telling the captain every mistake I make. I told him that I don't care about this S.O.R.T. crap, but since I was chosen for the position I would do the best I could do.

The next day the captain called me in his office and said he wanted to speak with me. I asked the captain what was wrong, and he proceeded to tell me the problem. The captain repeated everything verbatim that the activities lieutenant and I had spoken about the night before. Of course he was in the office, also. I asked the activities lieutenant if he told the captain about our conversation…he turned red and said he didn't know what I was talking about.

"You're a lie and you are a piece of shit! You'll never be a man. I am going to ask you again, did you discuss our conversation with the captain?"

He continued to deny it.

"Can I have a word with the lieutenant in private," I asked. "Yes," the captain said.

"I should kick your ass, but being that we are working I can't do that. From now on, follow my instructions!"

I held a meeting with the other members of the team, and told them if they undermine me along with the other lieutenant, they would be kicked off the team.

Those guys didn't want to be kicked off the team and I didn't want to be in charge of the team, but being that I was, I tried to do my best. All of the team members were in tiptop shape with the exception of me; I was in weightlifting shape.

Winning National Weightlifting Title

 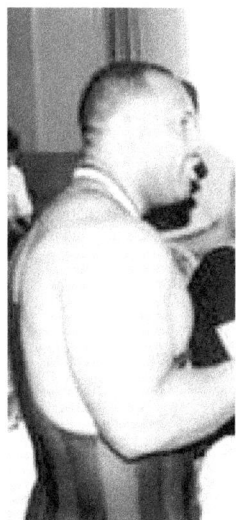

National Law Enforcement Games Weightlifting Competition

*Being Presented With A Gold Medal
For Bench Press (430 lbs.)*

When it came to running and playing Army or Marines, I wasn't with that, but this came with the territory. When we met in the gym to work out I was the head man in charge. These guys use to look at me with amazement on their face. While they were barely lifting two hundred and fifty pounds I was on the other bench playing with four hundred and five pounds, lifting it about three or four times in a row. My message to them without me saying a word was, 'Try me if you want to!' I think the guys got the message very quick.

The team and I started to gel a little bit, but I still didn't trust them any further than I could see them, even the black members on the team.

CHAPTER 21

Riots at F.C.I. Marianna

A month later, we started to hear rumors about this crack/powdered cocaine law. Of course I didn't know what this law was, but I soon found out.

The attorney general made a statement that congress was getting ready to change this racial law, because there was a study done by the United States Sentencing Commission that the law was biased and it affected more minorities than anyone else.

During the first week of October 1995, there were rumors around the bureau that congress was getting ready to pass an amendment to the Anti-Drug Abuse Act bill. This bill fell under the mandatory minimum law. If this bill passed, the inmates that were convicted and given long harsh sentences under the crack cocaine law, would possibly get their prison sentence reduced.

At the last hour, congress rejected the bill and several federal prisons went up in smoke (the inmates set the prisons on fire).

On October 18, 1995, while I was in the lieutenant's office working, I was summoned to the warden's office and told that the inmates were rioting at the Federal Correctional Institution in Marianna, Florida. The warden instructed me to take the Special Operation Response Team to Marianna, to assist the staff with the riot.

I called the control center and instructed them to call everyone on the S.O.R.T. team to meet me in the command center within the hour. The members loaded up the van with M-14's, 9- millimeters, stun guns, tear gas grenades, and riot gear.

FCI Marianna was one hour and ten minutes away from Tallahassee. The team and I arrived in Marianna, Florida in forty minutes. When we arrived we could see one dormitory on fire and inmates in the recreation yard throwing everything they could get their hands on to destroy the administrative building.

Needless to say, I felt as though, my heart was in my stomach, because I had a tough decision to make when I got inside the institution. If the inmates attack staff, other innocent inmates, or a certain area of the institution was breached; I had to give orders to shoot. If I gave orders to shoot, people were going to get hurt or lose their life. The riots went on, but no lives were lost.

While the S.O.R.T. and my team were in Marianna, Florida, I had a chance to hook up with my buddy I met in Denver named Darryl. He was the S.O.R.T. lieutenant in F.C.I. Marianna, Florida. It was ironic that two friends were the people in charge during the riots.

During the riots we kept a level head. Even though we knew the law was biased, and we knew why the inmates were fighting we still did our job. The weird thing about this entire ordeal was that the Bureau of Prisons called for a powerful black leader(Louis Farrakhan to try to convince the inmates from rioting.)The government hated Louis Farrakhan but I loved my brother. He spoke truth not hate, although I'm a Christian I have been following Farrakhan since I was in the 12th grade. The week before the Honorable Louis Farrakhan had just held the Million Man March in Washington, D.C. to promote African American and unity family values. This was a great march but the government said the Honorable Louis promoted hate which was not true.

Most people today are still not aware of how racist the mandatory minimum sentencing laws are. It is my obligation to break it down to my readers in layman's term where you can get a good understanding.

Mandatory minimum is a law that can take your nineteen-year-old son or your twenty-year-old daughter and send them to prison for twenty years, even though they've barely had a speeding ticket.

Now let me give you the definition of mandatory sentencing: They are prison terms required by law for certain crimes. For a particular crime, the judge *must* hand out at least a minimum amount of prison time, no matter the circumstances. This is mandatory. The judge has little to no discretion. A book/ chart dictates the amount of time. The laws come down especially hard on drug-related crimes.

Mandatory minimum sentences grew out of the War on Drugs in the 1980's. Worried about illegal drug use and drug crime, lawmakers passed tough, new laws to punish drug dealers.

The laws included long prison terms for people who aided drug dealers, even if the individual didn't make or sell drugs.

Mandatory minimum sentences were first introduced at the federal level in 1986 in an effort to incarcerate drug kingpins. However, a majority of criminals imprisoned for drug-related crimes have been street-level offenders. I should add in 1970, congress repealed most of the mandatory minimums, which had been part of the federal criminal justice system's sentencing structure.

The evidence clearly showed that increased sentence lengths were ineffective. The United States now has more than any other nation in the world, in the number of people behind bars. Many of them are nonviolent drug offenders. Including jail populations, as of 2002 America now incarcerates about 2.1 million people. One major factor behind the increases, have been the imposition of the mandatory minimum sentences contained in many federal laws, especially drug laws. A second reason for the rise is the effect of federal sentencing guidelines, which were adopted in the mid-1980's to make criminal sentences in federal cases more uniform.

Did you know almost one in three young black males are under some form of criminal supervision, either in prison or jail or on probation or parole? A Hispanic male born in 1991 has a one in six chance of spending time in prison. There are more young black men under criminal supervision than there are in college; for every one black male who graduates from college, over one hundred are arrested.

Although blacks make up only twelve percent of the U. S. population, they constitute 38 percent of those arrested for drugs, 59 percent of those convicted of drug offenses, and 74 percent of those sentenced to prison for a drug offense.

The Anti-Drug Abuse Act of 1986 provided mandatory minimum sentences of imprisonment for possession with to distribute powder and crack cocaine. In this statute congress established a quantitative 100-to-1-sentence ratio between the two (i.e., it takes one hundred times as much powder cocaine as crack cocaine to trigger the same sentence). Under this distinction, a person convicted of possession with the intent to distribute a pound of powder cocaine (453.6 grams)/street value worth forty- five thousand dollars would serve considerably less time in federal prison than one convicted of possession with intent to distribute five grams of crack/street value worth five hundred dollars.

Since the enactment of the amendment, the crack/powder sentencing differential has fallen disproportionately against African-Americans.

According to United States Sentencing Commission in 1994 the vast majority of persons convicted of crack possession were 84.5 percent Black. 10.3 percent White and 5.2 percent Hispanic. Trafficking crack offenders were 4.1 percent White, 88.3 percent Black and 7.1 percent Hispanic. Powder cocaine offenders were racially mixed.

Defendants convicted of simple possession of cocaine powder were 58 percent White, 26.7 percent Black, and 15 percent Hispanic. The result of the combined differences in sentencing laws and racial disparity is that black men and women are serving longer prison sentences than white men and women.

I might add since congress enacted its mandatory sentences for crack dealers in 1986, virtually all white offenders are prosecuted in state court, where sentences are far less, with differences of up to eight years for the same crime in federal court. In 1994 there was the Violent Crime Control and Law Enforcement Act that President Bill Clinton signed into law into on September 13, 1994. I called this act, the snitch act. The bill contained the so-called safety valve for low-level, nonviolent drug offenders. The way that it works is if the defendant can show that he meets five criterias spelled out in the law, and mimicked in the sentencing guidelines, basically no violence, no weapon, no aggravating role, no more than one criminal history, and tell all he knows about the offense to the government, then it lets the defendant out from under the mandatory minimums and allows the guidelines system to work with its mitigating factors that may apply.

As a result, the sentence may be reduced below the mandatory minimum. In the most extreme case, a snitch can tell a lie to save himself or herself from the mandatory minimum, by implementing another person in a crime that the person knew nothing about. Though this is the case, the government goes on the snitch's word. The other person is sent off to prison for something they didn't have anything to do with.

The implementation of The Violent Crime Control and Law Enforcement Act led prison population to soar by more than a million people, many disproportionately black and Latino because it significantly increased sentences for repeat offenders through a three-strikes provision which meted out a life sentence. Some may say the VCCLE caused mass incarceration, my answer to that is it added to the mass incarceration that was already in place prior to President Clinton signing The Violent Crime Control and Law Enforcement Act into law.

When my career began in the criminal justice system an inmate was able to apply for a Pell grant to continue their education. The Violent Crime Control and Law Enforcement Act effectively eliminated the ability of lower-income prison inmates to receive college educations during their term of imprisonment, thus ensuring the education level of most inmates remains unimproved over the period of their incarceration.

Thank God President Obama Administration had the insight to know in order to effect change in the penal system you have to create a fairer and more effective criminal justice system, reduce recidivism, and combat the impact of mass incarceration on families and communities through educational opportunity, with this being said, The Department of Education announced 67 colleges and universities selected to participate in the new Second Chance Pell pilot program, an experiment to test whether participation in high quality education programs increases after expanding access to financial aid for incarcerated individuals.

The pilot program will allow eligible incarcerated Americans to receive Pell Grants and pursue postsecondary education with the goal of helping them get jobs and support their families when they are released.

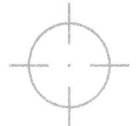

CHAPTER 22

Chaos after the Riot

Shortly after the riot, the institution remained chaotic amongst the staff and inmates. The inmates were on lock down in their cells. Only the inmates who worked in the food service department were allowed to work, because they had to prepare the food. Every movement was controlled, meaning the compound was not open, and the inmates could not come and go out of their dorms, unless approved. The Special Operations Response Team was located in the Wellness Center, with weapons and riot gear on 24 hours a day, just in case another disturbance kicked off. I was the Special Operations Response Team Lieutenant for the Federal Correctional Institution Tallahassee, and Anthony was the Special Operations Response Lieutenant for the Federal Correctional Institution Marianna. The inmates didn't know we were located at the Wellness Center, they assumed since the riots were over and everything was almost back to normal, the Tallahassee Special Operations Team had left.

We received intelligence from an inmate in Food Service, who claimed the other inmates that worked in Food Service were plotting a plan to kidnap a female worker, hold her hostage, and possibly rape her. We had to determine the best plan of action. We could have captured the inmates committing the kidnapping, or informed the food service staff member not to come to work. We chose the latter. The staff member didn't come to work, and the inmates figured out we had already gotten intelligence on their plan, so nothing kicked off.

I got tired of being stationed at the Wellness Center with full riot gear, including weapons and lack of sleep. When other staff members relieved us for four hours, Lieutenant Anthony and I went back to his house for a couple of hours to sleep on a comfortable bed. Lieutenant Darryl's wife cooked us a hot breakfast. We returned back to the institution, then relieved the staff that relieved us. After several days at F.C.I. Marianna, their institution returned back to normal, then my guys and I were able to return back to F.C.I. Tallahassee.

After returning back to F.C.I. Tallahassee, the Director of the Federal Bureau of Prisons made a decision to separate all the inmates who posed as leaders during the riots. He sent them to different parts of the country, where Federal Prisons were stationed. They tried to send them as far away as possible from their families. The culprits that were involved in the riots were sent to the East Coast, if they were from the West Coast, and vice versa. It's common practice to locate a prison close to where the inmates reside, to accommodate their family members. However, if an inmate receives a major infraction, that privilege goes out the window. Ironically, F.C.I. Tallahassee received some of the worst inmates in the bureau that were involved in the riots.

I hadn't been back in Tallahassee for 48 hours before the inmates arrived. After the inmates were processed, some of them said they didn't have shit to lose, and they were going to tear up everything in sight, including staff, if they could get to them. Needless to say, they were put in the Special Housing Unit (Lock-up). I can recall many incidents with these new inmates. I was working on the day shift when I got a call from Special Housing Unit that the inmates were chanting and banging on their cells in unison. One of the inmates also started flooding their cell. When I arrived, I informed the inmate in the flooded cell to step to the front and turn around so I could cuff him and move him to another cell. He said, "Fuck you, Lieutenant, I told you we were going to destroy this place."

The other inmates who were banging on the cells were chanting, "The white man sent you over to control us, you must be their flunky." Words never bothered me, I worked at some of the worst institutions, and that was standard language.

I asked the inmate one more time to come to the front, he said, "Motherfucker, I ain't coming anywhere, you bring your big ass in here to get me if you want me."

I said, "Look, homeboy, you are coming out of that cell one way or another. Now, which one is it going to be?"

The inmate said, "I'm not doing shit."

I immediately left the area, and the other inmates started laughing and said, "I thought you was a punk ass motherfucker." I made a phone call to the Control Center and told the officer I was sending someone over to retrieve the video camera. I also told the officers that were on shift to meet me at the office. Once they met me, I told them to go to the armory and put on their riot gear, minus their weapons, and to meet me over at the Special Housing Unit.

Some of the officers were saying, "What's going on, Lieutenant?"

I said, "We are going to do a force cell move." A force cell move is when we go inside a cell and remove an inmate by force. Once everyone was suited up, I explained to them what their instructions were, including the physician assistant. The physician assistant had to be there to render medical care to the inmate, and sometimes the officer.

I explained to the officers, "I am going to open the cell door, and you are all going in the cell to retrieve the inmate." I fully explained that multiple officers would grab the inmates upper left extremity, the bottom left extremity, the upper right extremity, lower right extremity, and one officer needed to hold the inmate down.

When I went back to the cell, the inmate said, "I see you brought your boys back, I wanted you to come and get me by yourself."

I said, "If it wasn't against policy, I would take care of you by myself." I explained to the inmate this was my last warning, "Come to the front of the cell and turn around where I can cuff you."

He said, "Come get me, motherfucker."

I turned around and told the cameraman to make sure the video was on, and I told the officers, "On my command, on three, I'm going to open the door and we are going to take care of business. 1, 2, 3, let's get him!" The officers went in the cell, and within 20 seconds, we were bringing the inmate out cuffed up and taking him to another cell. I asked the officers, "Are all of you all right?"

They said, "Yes, Lieutenant Jones, we're okay."

I asked, "Where is that blood coming from? There is a lot in the cell." When the inmate was placed in the cell and turned on his back, his face was swollen and bloody. I gave the physician assistant instructions to render medical care on the inmate, and told the officers to get washed up and return to their posts.

As I was leaving Special Housing Unit, one of the inmates said, "Lieutenant Jones, you will be back, because we don't have shit to lose. We aren't getting out because of those fucked up, racist, mandatory minimum laws."

CHAPTER 23

Burned Out

After I got off from work and went home for three hours, I got a call from the institution saying, "Lieutenant Jones, we have another uprising in Special Housing Unit."

I said, "You have a shift lieutenant and officers, why can't they handle it?"

They replied, "We have called other officers, but they aren't answering their phones."

"Okay, I will be there in a minute." I stayed in staff housing so I could see the institution from my house. If an emergency broke out, I would be the first called in.

When I arrived at the institution, the shift lieutenant briefed me on what was going on. He said, "I know you just left the institution a couple of hours ago, but I'm short staffed and I have to go finish my duties. You know how things work."

"Yeah, yeah. Whatever."

"We don't have enough officers to do a force cell move," he said.

"Shit," I replied, "I'm going to use whatever staff we have on duty then, including the Chaplain. Fill me in on what's going on, Lieutenant."

"I received a call from Special Housing Unit. The officer that was doing the feeding walked to cell 9 to give the inmate their dinner, and the inmate threw urine in his face."

"Okay, I will take it from here." I picked up my radio, "Lieutenant Jones to Control Center, I'm sending the compound officer to retrieve the video camera. Lieutenant Jones to Baker Unit, inform the Unit Manager to meet me in the armory. Lieutenant Jones to Delta Unit, inform the Unit Manager that he is working your unit. I need you to report to the armory. Lieutenant Jones to Charlie Unit, inform the case manager that he is working your unit. I need you to report to the armory. Lieutenant Jones to G-Unit, inform the counselor he is working your unit. I need you to meet me at the armory. Lieutenant Jones to the P.A., finish seeing the inmates and meet me at the unit. If you don't have a life-threatening crisis, then tell the inmates to report back to their units."

We all met at the armory to put on our riot gear and proceeded to Special Housing Unit. Once reaching the cell, the inmates said, "Lieutenant Jones, I told you that you'd be coming back, because we are going to destroy this place."

I informed everyone of which extremities they were to grab. I also said, "When I open the cell door, allow me to get it all the way open before you rush inside and break my arm." When we arrived to the cell door, I informed the cameraman to cut on the video and start filming. I proceeded to explain what the inmate did. "Inmate Harris assaulted an officer by throwing urine in his face. I have asked inmate Harris to step to the front of the cell and turn around so he can be cuffed, but inmate Harris has refused my orders. I have my staff present and we are going to extract inmate Harris from his cell and put him in another cell. My staff will introduce themselves and tell you what their responsibilities are. G-unit, what is your assignment?"

"Lieutenant Jones, I'm responsible for grabbing inmate Harris's top left extremity."

"Charlie Unit, what are your responsibilities?"

"Lieutenant Jones, I'm responsible for grabbing inmate Harris's bottom left extremity."

"Baker Unit, what are your responsibilities?"

"Lieutenant Jones, I'm responsible for grabbing inmate Harris's top right extremity."

"Delta Unit, what is your responsibility?"

"Lieutenant Jones, I'm responsible for grabbing inmate Harris's lower right extremity."

"Physician Assistant, what are your responsibilities?"

"Lieutenant Jones, I'm responsible for rendering medical assistance."

After everyone stated what their responsibilities were, I turned and looked at inmate Harris. He had already covered himself with feces. I said, "Inmate Harris, I'm giving you a direct order to step to the front of the cell door and turn around to be cuffed."

Harris said, "I'm not going to do a goddamn thing, you are going to have to come get me."

I turned to the staff and said, "On my command, we are going inside the cell to take inmate Harris down, 1, 2, 3, go!"

I opened the door, and the officers proceeded to take inmate Harris down. The inmate was slippery, and the staff had a hard time taking him down. When we finally got a hold of Harris, the staff informed me by stating, "G-unit has secured inmate Harris's top left extremity."

"Charlie Unit has secured inmate Harris's bottom left extremity."

"Baker Unit has secured inmate Harris's top right extremity."

"Delta Unit has secured inmate Harris's bottom right extremity."

I noticed inmate Harris's head bleeding. I informed the P.A. to render medical assistant.

I went back to the office to finish my report and informed the shift lieutenant that I was going home, because I had to be back at midnight, and it was already 8:30 PM. Before I left, I asked the shift lieutenant if the other staff members he called had responded. He said, "Yes, but all of them had been drinking."

"What about the captain?"

"He had been drinking," he said.

"I guess the staff has already figured out a way to not come in to help with emergencies, by saying they had been drinking. Bunch of cowards. They know we have a lot of shit going on, and these inmates are trying to destroy this institution, and their excuse for not coming in for an emergency is that they have been drinking?!" I replied angrily.

The shift lieutenant said, "Lieutenant Jones, take an extra hour tonight and come in at 1:00 AM. I will cover for you, I know you are tired." I said thanks and left.

I went home and caught a couple of hours of sleep. When I returned to the institution at 1:00 AM, I asked the shift lieutenant if things had been quiet since I left. He shook his head.

"I hope it stays that way," I replied.

He said, "You are working with the bare minimum staff, two more people called in sick while you were gone."

"Who is working the Special Housing Unit?"

"Harmon is working," he said.

"Oh shit, he is going to get those inmates in an uproar!" I called over to Special Housing Unit and informed Harmon not to start any shit with the inmates. "If they call you a name, just ignore it, because we don't have the staff to perform a force cell move. If the inmates are sleeping, let their asses sleep. Do you understand, Harmon?"

"Yes, sir, Lieutenant Jones, I understand. What time are you making your rounds tonight, sir?" Harmon asked.

"I don't know, but as long as those inmates are asleep, let them be."

I walked over to the P.A. office to see P.A. Stone working, he was an asshole and a racist. P.A. Stone came by my office for small talk and said, "I heard you've all been doing force cell moves all week, sometimes two and three times a day. These inmates are thugs." I looked at him and didn't say a word. He continued, "I have to go to Special Housing Unit at 6:00 AM to give some medication out."

I said, "Let me know before you leave, because I have to make my rounds."

It was 2:00 AM and my shift was going smoothly. 4:00 AM came around, and the shift was still going smoothly. I said to myself, "I might be able to get off work on time, since everything is quiet."

P.A. Stone came to the office and said, "Lieutenant Jones, it's almost 6:00 AM, are you ready to go to Special Housing Unit?"

I said, "Yes, let me put on my blazer."

While P.A. Stone and I were on our way to Special Housing Unit, I informed him that the inmates had been cursing at the staff when making their rounds. I told him to ignore that shit, give the inmates their medication, and then leave, so we could go home on time.

When P.A. Stone and I arrived to dispense medication, one of the inmates woke up and said, "Damn, Lieutenant, you work all the time, and who is this motherfucking cracker you have with you?"

P.A. Stone told the inmate if he was a cracker, then the inmate must be a nigger. Then the other inmates started waking up and cursing us out.

When P.A. Stone and I left, I looked at him and said, "Why in the hell did you call that inmate a nigger?"

"Well, he called me a cracker."

I said, "You have lost your damn mind if you think I'm not going to do anything about this incident. I expect the inmates to call us names, but I don't tolerate staff stooping so low. I expect staff to rise above that dumb shit. Now, we are going to be here all fucking morning doing paperwork." I told the P.A. I was going to write a memo and send it to the warden, informing him of what Stone called the inmate.

Stone said, "If a black inmate calls me a cracker again, then I'm going to call him a nigger."

"P.A. Stone, get the fuck out of my office, because you probably think I'm a nigger, too. If you ever slip and call me a nigger, then I'm going to bust your ass. You have always been a racist, and you know, the Bible states, what's in the heart, comes out the mouth."

After P.A. Stone left my office, I called his best friend, my captain, and informed him what happened. He came to the institution within five minutes, because he also stayed in staff housing. My captain didn't come because he was concerned about the P.A., he came because he knew I was getting ready to write a memo about the incident and send it to the warden. He knew I didn't play when it came to racism. When the captain came to my office, I could still smell the alcohol on his breath. After the captain read my memo, he asked me to delete a couple of things. I told him I wasn't deleting shit! He called P.A. Stone over to my office and asked us to shake hands. I shook his hand, but I still didn't change shit on the memo.

P.A. Stone looked at the captain and said, "Captain, are we still going fishing today?"

When the warden came in Monday morning and read the memo, he was pissed. He asked, "Garry, did this really happen?"

I told him yes. He said, "I'm referring this to internal affairs." I was relieved.

A couple of months later, internal affairs came to investigate the case and recommended P.A. Stone receive a week suspension without pay. The warden gave P.A. Stone two days on the street, because the union stepped in and helped him with his case.

CHAPTER 24

The Spark from the Light Gave Him Away

The following week, I asked the captain if I could be assigned to work the Federal Detention Center, so I could get a break. Normally, the Detention Center is the place that houses inmates who have already been sentenced, but are waiting to be assigned an institution. The inmates are also waiting for their trials. The inmates are allowed to watch television and play cards. The units have two television sets for sports or movies. The inmates have to vote on which sport programs they want to watch. The most trouble the staff will have is when the inmates vote on a program, and it's a tie. For example, the majority of the white inmates love to watch Nascar Racing, and the majority of the black inmates enjoy watching football or basketball. The staff breaks the tie.

The worst thing that can happen at a detention center is when a mistake is made when an inmate is assigned to the same unit where they snitched on another inmate in court. This mistake doesn't happen often, but when it does happen, this can create an atmosphere where an inmate is assaulted by the inmate they snitched on. Sometimes the inmates will tell the staff they need to be moved to another unit.

I can recall going to Special Housing Unit to make my rounds and sign my books, to ensure the inmates were getting what they were entitled to. I would go to each cell and talk with the inmates, because it was very important that I listened to what they had to say. Some staff would come in Special Housing Unit to sign the books but would not make the trip to speak with the inmates. They did this because they didn't want to be bombarded with questions. I was different, I knew a lot of trouble could be avoided if I spoke with the inmates and addressed their concerns. Inmates were entitled to one phone call a week in Special Housing Unit. If an inmate told me they didn't get their phone call, I would go back and check the books, and if I saw that the inmate was telling the truth, then I would instruct the officer to give the inmate a phone call. I went to one cell to talk with an inmate because he was suicidal. I asked the inmate whether or not he was getting everything, and he said yes. I asked if there was anything he wanted to talk with me about, and he said no, he wasn't up for any conversation. After making my rounds, I informed the officer to keep an eye on the inmate who was suicidal, because his conversation was short and he couldn't, or wouldn't, make eye contact with me.

I left Special Housing Unit to make my rounds to other units, and before I approached B-Unit, I received a call over the radio, "Lieutenant Jones, I need for you to report back to Special Housing Unit, we have an emergency. Please hurry, Lieutenant Jones."

When I got outside the door of Special Housing Unit, I told Control Center to open the door. I didn't know what the Control Center Officer was doing, but he took ten seconds to open the door. After getting inside the Special Housing Unit, I asked the officer what was going on. He said the inmate was cutting himself with a razor blade. I went to the inmate's cell, and he wasn't just cutting his body with superficial wounds, he was slicing and dicing his arms, and blood was shooting all over the cell. I instructed the officer to open the cell, and his hands were shaking so bad that he couldn't open it. I retrieved the keys, opened the door, and stopped the inmate from killing himself.

I picked up my radio and said, "Lieutenant Jones to Medical Service, I need medical assistance to Special Housing Unit ASAP." When the Physician Assistant arrived, he said the inmate's wounds were too deep for stitches. They had to transfer him to the medical office. When we got the inmate to medical services, the P.A. provided medical attention and said the inmate was not in that bad of shape. We took the inmate back to Special Housing Unit and he was bandaged up. I instructed the officer to shake down the cell the inmate was living in to search for the razor blade. I also instructed the officer to put him in another cell.

After the inmate got settled in his new cell, I asked the officer how in the hell the inmate got the razor blade, when he had supposedly been strip searched when he arrived in Special

Housing Unit. The officer claimed he didn't know. I went back and searched the logbook to find out how long the inmate had been in Special Housing Unit, and who the officer on duty was when the inmate arrived. After reviewing the logbook, I discovered the inmate had been in Special Housing for two weeks and had never caused any problem. I went back to the original cell to search for the razor blade, and I found the blade inside the mattress. I also retrieved the inmate's mail, and when I was reading the mail, I found a letter written by the inmate's wife stating she wanted a divorce. I understood then why the inmate didn't care about living.

I left Special Housing Unit, wrote up my report, and went home.

I made a conscious decision not to put the suicidal inmate in a cell with another inmate, because there was a possibility he could hurt his cellmate while his cellmate was sleeping. In my opinion, after reading the letter from his wife, he could now possibly be homicidal, but the psychiatrist had to determine that.

I went back to my office, wrote my report, and turned it in to the captain's office. The next two days I was off and I definitely needed the rest. I did my regular routine, I got some drinks, I worked out, played with Sparky the dog, and helped the kids out with their homework. I never discussed or brought my problems from work inside my house.

When I returned to work, I was informed by the shift lieutenant that the suicidal inmate was being transferred to another institution. I called the Special Housing Unit and told them to get the inmate ready to leave the unit.

I received a call from Special Housing Unit that the inmate claimed he wasn't going anywhere. I immediately left my office, went to the unit, and informed the inmate myself that he was being transferred.

He said, "Lieutenant Jones, I'm not going anywhere. If you want me, you are going to have to come in here to get me." I wasn't in the mood to go around and around with the inmate about him leaving the cell.

I said, "Come to the cell door and turn around so I can cuff you." He said no. I instructed the Control Center Officer to call the F.C.I. and tell the Operations Lieutenant to send me a team to the FDC to extract an inmate out of Special Housing Unit.

When the team arrived, I instructed them to go to R&D to suit up, and I gave everyone their instructions. I informed the Corridor Officer to get the video camera and meet me in R&D. I instructed the Control Center Officer to make an announcement that all inmate moving ceases. The team arrived outside Special Housing's door.

"Lieutenant Jones to the Control Center, open the Special Housing Unit door." When the Control Center Officer opened the door, I looked at my team and said, "When I open this cell door, don't break my damn arm, I know how aggressive you all can get."

I could look in my team's eyes and tell they were ready for action. I said, "Team, we are going to use the minimum amount of force as possible to get the job done. Once he is down, if he complies with the orders and is no longer trying to squirm his way out, then do not apply any force, just cuff him and get him out of the cell."

The team's momentum could be so high they forgot they were being recorded.

As we were walking towards the inmate's cell, I could hear him saying, "Come get me, motherfuckers." When we approached his cell, he was already slicing and dicing his whole body again. I was not expecting that, I opened the cell door and body slammed him to the floor. The team cuffed him. I told the Special Housing Unit Officer to find the razor blade. The inmate's cell was covered in so much blood, it was as if he cut an artery.

We took the inmate to R&D and called the P.A. over to render medical assistance. I received a call from the Special Housing Unit Officer, and they informed me that they couldn't find the razor blade. I asked the inmate where the blade was, but he refused to answer. I instructed one of the officers to shake him down, but they were also unable to find the blade. The P.A. said they may have to take him out to the local hospital. I told them that was okay, but I was going to find that blade. I asked the inmate to open his mouth, and to lift his tongue up and down, he complied. I asked him to move his tongue to the left and right, he complied, and before I could ask the inmate to say "awwww," the light from the ceiling shined on an object in his mouth and made it sparkle. That's when I saw the blade.

The inmate's eyes made contact with mine, and he realized that I spotted the blade. He tried to swallow it, but I grabbed his neck and attempted to choke it out. He realized the only way I was going to get that blade out of his mouth was by squeezing his neck as hard as possible, in order to keep him from swallowing. I did just that, and while the inmate was choking, I also did a dangerous move. I took my right hand, put it in the inmate's mouth, and gently removed the blade. Blood was gushing from his mouth and splashing on the face shield of my helmet. After the blade was retrieved, the inmate started choking and couldn't breathe. I thought he was choking from the blood, but we discovered later on that I almost broke his windpipe, and that was why he was choking.

After this ordeal was over, the inmate continued to receive medical attention, and eventually, he was transferred to another institution.

CHAPTER 25

F. Lee Bailey

Shortly after fighting in the riots October 1995 and the news of O.J. Simpson being found not guilty of murder, I had to face another battle, namely dealing with high profile inmates. I have worked several institutions where high profile inmates were incarcerated, and often some rules just didn't apply to them. I can recall this high profile lawyer who would come to the institution to visit an inmate he was representing from time to time, but after he was assigned to the dream team of lawyers who represented O.J. Simpson he became bigger than life.

To a lot of people, if it wasn't for him cross examining the state's main witness and catching him in a lie, causing that witness to eventually plead the fifth, O.J. Simpson may have been found guilty for the murder of Nicole Brown Simpson and Ron Goldman. The attorney I'm talking about is F. Lee Bailey. He was a prominent lawyer back in the 60s and the 70s, representing high profile clients such as Sam Sheppard, Albert

DeSalvo, and Patty Hearst. Some of you probably wouldn't remember these clients because you were either to young or weren't even born at all.

Sam Shepherd was a neurosurgeon initially convicted for the 1954 murder of his wife, Marilyn Sheppard. He was sentenced to life in prison, but after F. Lee Bailey took up the case in 1964 Sheppard was given a retrial, and he was released from prison on November 16, 1966.

Albert DeSalvo was a criminal in Boston, Massachusetts, who confessed to being the "Boston Strangler," the murderer of 13 women in the Boston area from 1962 to 1964. DeSalvo was already in prison for a series of rapes, but he confessed to killing the 13 women to another inmate, who eventually told F. Lee Bailey, who then took on DeSalvo's case. Bailey tried to get his client off by saying he was not guilty of the sexual offenses by reason of insanity. That defense was ruled inadmissible by the judge, and in 1967 DeSalvo was sentenced to life in prison. DeSalvo was never charged for a crime related to the deaths of the 13 women. He was, however, later found dead in his cell under mysterious circumstances.

Patty Hearst was a newspaper heiress who had committed armed robberies after being kidnapped by the Symbionese Liberation Army. Though she was originally a victim of the SLA, Hearst later drove one of their getaway cars during a robbery. A customer was killed when one of the robber's guns discharged. The SLA members participating in the robbery were therefore subject to the death penalty. Bailey was able to negotiate a plea agreement with the prosecutorsin which, in exchanger her testimony about the robbery, she would be protected from a death sentence. Hearst was convicted and sentenced to seven years in prison. She served 22 months before her sentence was commuted by President Jimmy Carter in 1977. She was pardoned by Bill Clinton in 2001.

Eventually, F. Lee Bailey would find himself on the other side of the law and have to deal with Lieutenant Jones and the Federal Bureau of Prisons's rules.

Shortly after 4:30 p.m. on March 07, 1996, Mr. Bailey turned himself in to Federal Marshals in Tallahassee to begin serving a six-month term on a civil contempt order. Under the terms of the order, Mr. Bailey could not be released until he served the six months or produced about $3 million in cash, and stock worth about $18 million.

There were times I didn't know whether or not the Federal Bureau of Prisons was following the rules with F. Lee Bailey. On my days off Inmate Bailey was getting a few things that weren't authorized, but when I came back to work things fell back into place and he was treated like any other inmate.

I can recall making rounds in A-Unit at the Federal Detention Center in Tallahassee, Florida. I was the shift Lieutenant on duty. I heard over the radio that an inmate was being released from the Special Housing Unit. That was odd because the Lieutenant only duty has to authorize any inmate moves for security reasons. I called Officer Chuck and asked who he released. He said, " F. Lee Bailey."

I asked, "Who authorized the move, Officer Chuck?"

"The unit manager wanted to see him, Lieutenant Jones."

"Officer Chuck," I continued, "do you know the protocol when releasing an inmate from Special Housing Unit?" Officer Chuck was silent. I asked again.

"Yes, Lieutenant, I was supposed to notify you."

"Why didn't you, Officer Chuck?"

"It wasn't a big deal, Lieutenant Jones."

I told him, "Officer Chuck I will deal with you later on. You just violated security protocol."

I proceeded to Unit Manager Jenkins's office, and F. Lee Bailey and Officer Jenkins were laughing and drinking coffee. I asked, "Jenkins do you know F. Lee Bailey is a security risk and the shift Lieutenant has to be notified when he is moved."

Jenkins responded, "Lieutenant Jones, I needed him to sign some paperwork."

"Jenkins why in the hell you didn't you get off your lazy ass and go to Special Housing Unit to have inmate Bailey to sign the paperwork?" Jenkins's face turned red, and he stared at me as if he was surprised. "As a matter of fact, why isn't inmate Bailey in restraints? If inmate Bailey jumped up and knocked the shit out of you, you would think he done you wrong, but you know all inmates coming from Special Housing Unit are supposed to be in restraints." Jenkins knew the proper protocol when releasing an inmate from Special Housing Unit because before he worked as a unit manager. He had also worked in security.

What was really happening was that Jenkins wanted to have F. Lee Bailey in his office by himself so he could go home and chat with the people in the streets, telling them that he and F. Lee Bailey were drinking coffee together in his office.

We had already received word from the Central Office that anyone is caught taking a picture of F. Lee Bailey in his orange jumpsuit would be fired. The reason was that some media outlet was paying one million dollars for the picture because F. Lee Bailey was high profile and famous for representing O.J. Simpson in the murder trial of Nicole Brown Simpson and Ron Goldman. The media were paying top dollar to embarrass F. Lee Bailey because O.J. Simpson was found not guilty, and the country was divided, and O.J. Simpson's attorneys were hated by a lot of people who thought O.J. Simpson was guilty of the murder. One of the main reasons that F. Lee Baily was in the Special Housing Unit in the first place was the fear that someone might try to kill him due to that same hatred.

I called the corridor officer on the radio to have him meet me at Jenkins's office in order to escort Bailey back to his cell, and then I went to the office to counsel officer Chuck for not informing me that F. Lee Bailey was leaving Special Housing Unit and not putting him in restraints before taking him from the Special Housing Unit. Two weeks later, while I was making my rounds in the Special Housing Unit, I heard what I thought was someone typing on a typewriter. When I got to Inmate Bailey's cell, inmate Bailey was, indeed, pecking away on a typewriter. Officer James was the Special Housing Unit officer that day.

I asked Officer James, "Who in the hell authorized inmate Bailey to have a typewriter in his cell?" Officer James didn't say anything. "Answer me, God damn it!"

Finally, he said, "Lieutenant Jones, the typewriter was already in the cell when I relieved the officer from duty to take over my shift."

"Officer James, is there a memo authorizing this typewriter in an inmate cell?

"No, Lieutenant Jones, there is not."

"Well, Officer James, take that typewriter out of Inmate Bailey's cell."

Inmate Bailey looked at me and went to sit on his bed, but he made a show of writing down my name on a pad as if to intimidate me. I went back to Officer James's office and apologized to him for using foul language. I explained to Officer James that people were authorizing F. Lee Bailey to have unauthorized things, but they were not putting it in writing. "It's okay for F. Lee Bailey to have certain things if it is in writing," I explained. "Do you understand, Officer James?"

"Yes, Lieutenant Jones."

"Officer James, do you realize whose head is going to roll when the Captain finds out F. Lee Bailey is being given unauthorized equipment?"

"Who, Lieutenant Jones?"

"I have to take the heat because I'm responsible for security." I didn't discipline Officer James because I try to build officer morale, not tear it down. Later on, I found out that the Captain knew F. Lee Bailey had a typewriter in his cell but was afraid to put the authorization in writing. When one inmate is being treated different than another inmate, that's where tension rises and other inmates start lashing out, demanding to be treated the same way.

The next week Inmate Bailey had a visitor, and he was released from the Special Housing Unit to go see his visitor, but he had to submit to a strip search going in to see his visitor and again when he came out. F. Lee Bailey didn't want to submit to a strip search. I informed the officers that if he didn't submit to a strip search they could take him back to his cell. Bailey was pissed. He wanted to see his visitors. It's ironic because prior to being incarcerated Bailey would come see his client, Inmate Dubac, and now he was the one in the orange suit. Another big reason security was tight on F. Lee Bailey was because his client was at the same Detention Center and we had to make sure they never crossed paths.

On April 20, 1996 F. Lee Bailey was released from Federal Detention Center Tallahassee after serving six weeks for contempt of court. The lawyer had a year to pay the Government $700,000, but he said that he intended to get it back, and more, through the courts.

"I'm going to go get my money back with a lawsuit, like everyone in a civilized world."

Mr. Bailey told reporters at the Tallahassee airport shortly before boarding his four-seat, twin-engine Piper airplane to return to his home near West Palm Beach.

According to the New York Times, Bailey told reporters, "I feel it was unnecessary" adding that he felt he'd been 'steam rolled' by Federal prosecutors who wanted to obtain Baily's stock, which had increased in value from $5.9 million to about $16 million since 1994.

CHAPTER 26

David Anthony Mack # 12866-112

When I reported to work one morning and attended a meeting, I was given information that David Mack would be in the Special Housing Unit. He had just arrived the night before. I knew the name sounded familiar, but surely they be couldn't be talking about the police officer allegedly involved in the killing of Christopher "The Notorious B.I.G." Wallace.

FBI papers obtained through a Freedom of Information Act request detail the L.A. Police Department's investigation of the 1997 fatal shooting of Christopher Wallace. They also imply the involvement of now former police officer David Mack—a revelation that left the public in shock. On March 09, 1997—just six months after Tupac Shakur's murder in Las Vegas—Biggie and his crew were leaving a party at the L.A.'s Peterson Automotive Museum in a three-cararavan when a black

Chevy SS Impala pulled up to his window and fired several shots, killing Biggie instantly.

According to the FBI investigation, the bullets used in the shooting were metal piercing Gecko 9mm bullets, which are manufactured in Germany and only available in the U.S. through two distributors. After Biggie's death David Mack was arrested for masterminding a Bank of American heist of over $700,000. I bet you are wondering what the hell a bank robbery has to do with who killed Biggie. When the police suspected Mack of robbing the bank, they raided his house and found both Gecko ammunition and a shrine to Tupac. They also spotted a black Chevy SS Impala parked next to Mack's house: The bullets and the car appeared to match those from the scene of Biggie's murder.

An L.A.P.D. detective named Russel Poole also investigated Biggie Smalls' death, and he came up with a theory that three police officers were responsible for the murder along with the CEO of Death Row Records, Suge Knight. David Mack was one of the three police officers that Poole had linked to the murder. Officer Mack had allegedly worked as a Suge Knight bodyguard. Investigator Poole suggested that Mack and Knight conspired to kill Smalls in retaliation for the murder of Tupac Shakur. Suge Knight was never implicated in Small's murder, but in 1997 he was sentenced to nine years in prison on a parole violation. Poole was eventually told to drop his investigation.

David Mack has always denied being involved with the murder of Biggie Smalls, and he didn't come to Federal Detention Center Tallahassee for a conspiring to murder him. He was here on some other dumb shit—and I mean dumb.

Mack was eventually convicted of robbing a bank and sentenced to 14 years in Federal Prison. Can you imagine a police officer robbing a bank? Nevertheless, he was at our institution, and we were responsible for keeping him safe.

Whenever the Bureau of Prisons receives ex-Law Enforcement officers who have gotten in trouble with the law and sentenced to prison they are often put into Special Housing Unit (SHU, aka "lockup") until it is deemed safe to for the individuals to mingle with the regular population.

After the meeting in which I was briefed about Inmate Mack, I went to the Special Housing Unit to check on him. He was very polite when I spoke with him. He looked worried, and I could see why: He was an ex law enforcement officer, word on the street was that he had something to do with Biggie being killed, and now he was in prison with some of Biggie's fans. I knew that while he was in Tallahassee Mack would never be close to any inmates, including in his cell. In order to keep high profile inmates safe, it is important for officers to implement proper security procedures because inmates are waiting to get a chance to go after their target.

Those inmates study each and every officer to see which ones slip and don't follow the proper security procedures. One slip up and an inmate can be attacked and die within a matter of seconds. A week after he arrived inmate Mack was transferred to a Federal Detention Center in Miami, Florida. It wouldn't be the last time he moved.

In 2001, while serving time at a Federal Prison in Illinois, David Mack was attacked and suffered a puncture wound to one of his lungs. Just like with those security procedures, it's very important to me to play by the right rules. Unfortunately, I would later suffer through retaliation because I refused to bow down to what was wrong, because I refused to turn my head.

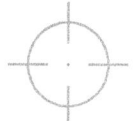

CHAPTER 27

Racial Disparities/Federal Parole

The United States Sentencing Commission found that nearly 90 percent of the offenders convicted in federal court for crack cocaine offenses are African American; despite federal surveys that routinely show that the majority of crack users are white.

In addition to these racial disparities, commentators have found that mandatory minimums lead to lengthy sentences for low-level drug dealers, fail to target violent criminals, and *do not* have a deterrent effect on major drug traffickers. The Sentencing Reform Act of 1984, which established determinate sentencing, abolished parole, and reduced good time, as well as mandatory minimum sentences for drug and weapon offenses and increases in prosecution and convictions, all have given rise to a dramatic increase in the federal inmate population.

After examining the disparity in the sentencing issue, the United States Sentencing Commission, following a public hearing on March 14, 1995, voted 4-3 to eliminate the disparity between conditions of possession of crack and powder cocaine. On May 1, 1995, the Commission proposed and sent to congress an amendment (providing for a 1:1 ratio) to the federal sentencing guidelines that would equate crack and powder cocaine for sentencing purposes.

The United State Sentencing Commission specifically suggested that Congress should take the 100-to-1 ratios from its own mandatory minimum penalties found in current statues. With the Commission's recommendations scheduled to become law on November 1, 1995, congress rejected the one to one ratio in the proposed amendment on October 30, 1995, which is why nine federal prisons went up in smoke and I had to lead the S.O.R.T. to a riot in Marianna, Florida.

I do not uphold any involvement with drugs of any sort, but at the same time, I do not support a system that sends a twenty-one year old to prison for twenty-three years for a drug charge.

If there is any story that tells the injustice in our criminal justice system, it is this story. Vanessa Wade (a black female) received twenty-three years for a non-violent offense.

After Vanessa mother committed suicide, she felt responsible for her younger siblings and fell victim to an older man that assisted her to the path of destruction. This is what a drug kingpin does; they find someone that is vulnerable, in need and recruit.

Vanessa was only nineteen years old at the time, while this drug kingpin was ten years her senior.

They tried her as a lieutenant, because they say she supervised a seventeen-year old youth. She was convicted of conspiracy to distribute and possession with intent to distribute cocaine.

The police didn't want Vanessa ; they wanted the kingpin, her boyfriend. Instead of getting her boyfriend, she received twenty-three years without parole in federal prison for a non-violent offense of twenty grams of cocaine base, while her boyfriend, the kingpin, walked free.

I don't know how much twenty grams of cocaine base was at the time, but it couldn't have been any more than fifteen hundred dollars back then. I am more than sure a person can get twenty grams of cocaine for about three or four hundred dollars in the streets today.

While Vanessa was incarcerated, her brother was accepted into Bethune Cookman College, but he never made it. He got in an argument with this young kid; later the kid came back and shot him in the head. The guy that shot and killed her brother was out of prison within two years for a violent offense...murder.

This was a terrible blow for her, because if she had been there, it is believed this crime would never have taken place. She had to be escorted to her brother's funeral by bureau staff in shackles. Now Vanessa is left with no mother, no father, and no brother.

I'm not an advocate for getting rid of prisons; that would be absurd. When the mandatory minimum sentencing was created in 1970 it was to get the hardened criminals off the street, but the non-violent offenders suffer just like the hardened criminals.

The Sentencing Reform Act of 1984 was created to abolish parole and reinstate the mandatory minimum. It didn't work in 1970 and it's not working now.

I can tell you one thing that the Reform Act of 1984 has done, it has destroyed not just the individual, but the reform act is destroying families. These laws are a travesty, it's inhumane to sentence non-violent offenders to a large amount of time and throw the key away.

How can you give a non-murderer, a non-rapist, a non-child molester, such a lengthy sentence and tell them they have to serve every minute of it? The individual that is suffering is the inmate himself/herself, because he or she feels like they don't have to obey the rules and regulations when they arrive to prison.

In their minds they are thinking, 'Why should I try to change my life when no matter what I do be it good or bad, I have to serve the entire sentence.' The inmate is not given an incentive to try to do right. How many of you would like it if Jesus decided not to give you a second chance. We would all be doomed. Who is without sin, throw the first stone.

It's nothing wrong with trying out an idea, but when your idea is not working try something new. This mandatory minimum sentencing is not working. We have tried this law for almost twenty years and it didn't work. We tried it in 1970 and it didn't work. Now we need to try to reinstate federal parole, retroactively.

There is another drug that is on the rise and it is causing an epidemic. This drug is called meth. This drug is not as popular of a drug of choice amongst black people. Meth is a drug epidemic that is on the rise amongst white people. I am not in favor of *any* drugs, but I cannot help but notice how the government is moving at a very fast pace to get treatment programs and centers for meth users, and how the government is taking ingredients used to make this drug off open counters in stores, placing them behind the counters to keep white people from making this illegal drug.

The government is doing whatever they can, to protect, treat, and detour whites from this illegal drug, but when crack was on the rise the government took no such measures, instead blacks were sent straight to jail for ten, twenty, and/or thirty years to life without parole!

Skin color should not determine how justice is carried out, but folks the facts speak for themselves…skin color does determine who goes to jail and who does not!

CHAPTER 28

Working for a New Supervisor and a New Warden

Shortly after the riots were over, I resigned as the Special Operations Response Team lieutenant. The activities lieutenant as well as the Captain, were still undermining me. I informed the captain that I did not want to work as the S.O.R.T. lieutenant anymore. Deep down inside the captain was elated. He found another lieutenant that didn't have any problems working my position.

One of my friends the warden promoted to come to the Federal Correctional Institution was named, Lieutenant Dee. He and I were friends from the Federal Prison Camp at Seymour Johnson Air Force Base. He was a military man, and knew all about being a S.O.R.T. lieutenant. The captain had what he wanted or at least he thought he had what he wanted. The captain never wanted me in the position and being that Dee knew about being a S.O.R.T. lieutenant, Dee replaced me.

Even though he was a white lieutenant, I never felt like he was a racist; to this day Lieutenant Dee never said anything around me to make me think he was a racist.

After I explained to the warden why I was stepping down, he made sure the captain removed activities S.O.R.T. lieutenant from his position. The captain was furious, but he didn't have any other choice but to follow the orders of the warden.

There was at least one time during the year that the S.O.R.T. teams from different regions competed against each other for bragging rights. This competition was held in South Carolina that year. The team from Tallahassee was expected to win the competition. Whenever these competitions were held, the captain from the institution would take the team to the competition.

A couple of days later, I received word that some trouble had taken place. I heard that the captain and the black lieutenant went to pick up some liquor at the liquor store. Even though nothing was wrong with that…I drank liquor myself, these two idiots went to the liquor store in the government vehicle to purchase the liquor. You can't have alcohol in the government vehicle.

When the S.O.R.T. team came back to Tallahassee, they had to be dealt with, mainly the captain because he was the leader. The warden immediately removed the captain from his position and Internal Affairs conducted an investigation.

We had an acting captain during the time this investigation took place. After the investigation was over, the captain was demoted to a lieutenant and transferred to an institution in Minnesota and the black lieutenant was transferred to an institution in Pennsylvania. The black lieutenant received a promotion as a unit manager, because he snitched on the captain.

Shortly after the investigation was over, the warden received word that he was going to the United States Penitentiary in Oklahoma. A black female was promoted to captain, and arrived at F.C.I. Tallahassee. Before she arrived at the institution, the 'all male' inmates institution was converted to 'all female' inmates institution. The only male inmates we had were located at the Federal Detention Center, which is located next door to the institution. Everyone was wondering with Mr. Flowers (the warden) being gone, what would happen to me. I wasn't worrying about a thing. I knew my position. Mr. Flowers equipped me with knowledge, and I had taken and completed sixteen Cross Development Courses. I knew the in's and the out's of every department of the institution. Normally, the associate warden took Cross Development Courses, although eventually anyone could take the courses. It appeared no one wanted to get any knowledge.

CHAPTER 29

The Captain from Hell

Earlier I mentioned the institution promoted a black female captain. She was one of the first two captains from hell that I had to work for. I received a call from one of my home girls that worked as a unit manager at the Federal Correctional Institution in Butner, North Carolina.

She told me that the black female captain that was promoted to Tallahassee was from our hometown in Kinston, North Carolina. Of course I didn't know her. My home girl (Olivia), told me to make sure the captain didn't fail at her position. She wanted me to give the captain the scoop on everything that went on in Tallahassee, and let her know who the enemies were that would cross her up in her new position.

I remember going to meet the captain and her husband at Super 8 Motel in Tallahassee, Florida. When I met with her, I had bad vibes, but since Olivia and I were close friends, I did what she asked me to do. The bad vibes I had about the captain would soon come to fruition.

After working for the captain, she reminded me of a house Negro. In my humble opinion she thought white was right, and everything and everyone who was black didn't know anything. She treated me worse than the white captain had. She was also a big liar. I remember telling her at the hotel that I didn't want or need anything from her. I was doing Olivia a favor by helping her out. I told her I wasn't leaving Tallahassee until my daughter graduated from high school.

There were so many incidents happening in Tallahassee, that weren't according to policy and procedure that were downright disrespectful and undermining.

On one occasion when I came to work, I was short on staff. I only had one officer working on the compound (location outside of housing units for inmates).

I had two control center officers. Therefore, I needed another person on the compound. I decided to vacate control #2 to provide coverage on the compound, because the person as control #1 was a senior officer specialist and could handle control by herself.

So I took control #2 and asked him to work on the compound.

He stated, "I don't want to go work on the compound, I'm going home sick if I have to work on the compound."

I said to him again, "You know you are being reassigned to the compound?"

"I am going home sick."

He took off without getting permission to go home sick. I called the captain (from hell…Sullivan) and informed her and Montana…the A.W (Associate Warden), what had just taken place. She called the front lobby, told Mrs. Thaxton to stop him in the parking lot, and told him to come to the office.

He refused to come to the office; he just went to his car and went home.

The next day I wrote a memo in reference to everything that transpired and sent it to the captain; nothing was ever done about it. A couple weeks later, after I asked the captain what was going on with the incident, she told me she decided not to pursue the incident with Jack Sutton, because that might make him lose his job.

The fact that he undermined me as a supervisor, by deciding not to do what I told him to do, makes the next person think they can do the same thing. Am I right or wrong?

If an officer gets sick on the job, the officer has to call the lieutenant and say, 'Look I'm sick. I'm not feeling well.' Every now and then the lieutenant might send the officer to the Physician Assistant (of the medical department), and let the P.A. check him or her out, if they are already at work. This particular officer just got in his car and left without being properly relieved; it all stemmed from my need for him to work the compound, a post he didn't want to work.

This same thing happened to a white lieutenant. A black the officer walked out on a white lieutenant without being properly relieved, saying he was going home sick. The captain supported the white lieutenant's disciplinary report on the black officer, but she did not do this with me, as a black lieutenant when I wrote a disciplinary report on the white officer for doing the exact same thing, (blatantly undermining my authority by getting in his car and leaving work).

One evening on the 4:00 p.m. to 12:00 a.m. shift, Officer Hood (a black officer) failed to inventory some property of an inmate. Officer Hood was an exceptional officer. The captain found out about it and informed me that I needed to write her up, because she is tired of officers failing to perform their duties.

She said, "I am going to make an example out of Hood."

I reluctantly wrote it. I had to do what my supervisor (the captain) told me to do. When I wrote a memo discipling officer Hood I wrote a halfass memo eventually the disciplinary report was thrown out.

About two months later, *I* informed Officer Bradshaw to inventory some property, because an inmate was going over to special housing (Lock-up) from his unit.

He stated, "I am not going to inventory the property, because I don't have time."

So when I went to the captain in reference to disciplining him, she stated, "No, just counsel him." Why didn't she let me counsel the other officer (Hood), when she did the same thing, only 2 months before?

Instead, she said, "Give him (Officer Bradshaw) a break." She was still undermining me as a lieutenant.

As a lieutenant, supervising officers, I have always tried to think of ways to build morale on my shift; therefore, I coordinated with another supervisor and decided to give a shift party for the day shift officers.

We wrote out the directions on how to get to one lieutenant's house where the party would be held. The directions were placed in everybody's box. Everybody that was a day shift officer was invited, and we opened it up to others that did not work day shift…whites, blacks and Hispanics. The main purpose of the party was to award the officers for a job well done, for the quarter, and we wanted to continue to build their morale.

We had the party at Lieutenant Caldwell's house sometime in October on a Friday. Monday when I got to work, the captain called me in her office, saying, 'I called you in reference to having a 'race' party, just black people were invited and not the whites."

"No, this was a shift party, *everyone* was invited.

Everyone on day shift received an invitation, if it was a 'race' party, why did Officer Bradshaw show up with his wife; both of them are white? Why are you questioning me?"

"Well, if you have a party, you should have a party for everybody."

"No, I shouldn't have a party for everybody. I was letting the officers on day shift know I appreciate the work they'd done."

It was a *shift* party, as I stated earlier, anyone who was not working that day was invited, plus this was at someone else's house; it wasn't on bureau property, and we paid our own money.

"You can't tell me what to do with my money off institution property."

She never questioned the white lieutenants in reference to the party we had for DCT (Disturbance Control Team) all the time. She never questioned them about parties, but she wanted to get on my case and accuse me of trying to do a 'race' party...she started harassing me.

Every time I turned around there was something with this captain from hell...

As a supervisor working 4:00 p.m. to 12:00 a.m. (evening shift) the psychologist came over to me and said, "We have an inmate, that's hearing voices over there in D Unit"...

I asked, "Is she a threat to the compound?"... "She could be"...Doctor House says.

"Well, as a supervisor I am going to see if we can get her locked up, so she won't harm anyone. You need to go ahead and do some type of testing on this inmate Dr. House, this was the end of the shift and Dr. House and other staff members were in a rush to go home. Telling me this type of news while walking out the door going home was not the type of news I wanted to hear. They should have called us earlier about this inmate; as soon as they received the information that she was hearing voices.

I said, "Well, we need to do something, either we put her on 'suicide watch' - this is where the inmate is locked in a room to protect them from harming themselves and/or others, while they are watched by another inmate, that sits outside of the room door to insure they don't hurt themselves - or I can just try to lock her up"...

"Well, I don't think she needs to be in special housing unit.

I said, "But you are telling me that we have an inmate that's hearing voices, you don't know what she is going to do... as the supervisor, I think I should take the appropriate action and try to do something. The unit manager Carol Townsend is telling me the only thing the inmate is going to do when she hears voices, is run down the compound with her clothes off."

I said, "Okay, let me go tell the captain and the A.W. what's going on." I told the captain I didn't feel comfortable with the inmate being left on the compound; especially with the things the psychologist had just told me.

The captain said, "I'm going to talk to the psychologist."

But she never got back with me, so I called the captain again, "What are we going to do about inmate Blue?

She just played it off like, 'The psychologist keeps saying he is going to get back with me.'

I said, "Okay, okay"...

In the meantime, everybody goes home. I told the psychologist, "I would hate to call y'all in another hour and a half if this inmate does something." "We need to start trying to take action now before something happens."

5:30 p.m. inmate Blue who resides in Delta unit began hearing voices; she jumps off the top bunk and starts choking this other inmate (an old white lady), trying to beat the crap out of her.

I called and notified the appropriate personnel (the captain), explaining to her that this is the incident that I was trying to keep from happening, but I didn't get any support. If she'd let me run my shift as a supervisor and let me lock this inmate up, this action would never have taken place.

The captain caused another inmate's life to be in danger.

Inmate Blue almost killed that old white lady when she jumped off her bunk beating that inmate. She was over three hundred pounds. I knew how inmate Blue could get when she hadn't taken her medication, but the captain would not listen.

CHAPTER 30

Food Strike at Tallahassee

There were rumors that the female inmates were planning on conducting a food strike at the institution, not because they thought the food was bad, but they were mad because they had to send a lot of their personal items home.

When the new warden and the captain arrived, they allowed the female inmates to have a lot of personal property, which was against policy. When the warden decided to take the inmate personal property or give them a chance to send the property home the inmates got mad. They had to send a lot of their jewelry home.

It's important that you follow policy and procedures when working in a prison, never allow inmates to have what they're not supposed to have, then turn around and try to take it back. This will cause problems every time.

There were warning signs that the inmates were going forward with the food strike. The commissary was selling food in record numbers. The inmates were storing up the food, in their personal storage areas, because they already had it in their minds, they weren't going to go to the dining hall to eat when the food strike started. The staff in the commissary should have alerted the administration that they were selling food in record numbers.

Even if the alert had been given to the new warden, he wouldn't have taken the staff's advice. He thought he was very intelligent and he also thought he knew it all.

Of course the warden didn't like me anyway, because he didn't like the former warden, so he took his frustration out on every staff member that the former warden had hired. This new warden wanted to take me down real bad, but the fact that I knew my job made it hard for him to do. I didn't give him this opportunity.

I remember working out at the gym one day; the new warden was in there. He knew the prior warden and I were friends so he would speak very negative of him, but I didn't fall for his tricks. Every time he spoke *negative* of him, I would speak *positive* of him.

Getting back to the food strike, I remember it like it was yesterday. One of my friends was in the lieutenant's office one foggy evening. My friend's name was Robert. Robert would often come by the institution after he was relieved from his shift to talk with me. He was due to go to Denver the next day for special investigative training.

It was a Saturday evening when an inmate came to the lieutenant's office. This particular inmate would talk with us a lot. Whenever we worked she would come to the lieutenant's office. This time, she informed us about the food strike that we heard was going to take place. She told Robert and I that she knew who the ringleaders were in every dorm.

This was good information, because I like to be proactive. Being proactive would cause fewer problems for a person in the future. I remember Robert telling me that he had to go back to the house and finish packing. I told Robert that I would inform the captain about the information I'd received.

I called the captain at home and asked her if I could lock up the ringleaders of the dorm that were going to conduct the food strike. I informed the captain that I believed if she gave me permission to lock up the ringleaders, we could prevent the food strike from happening.

The captain stated she didn't think the food strike was going to take place. She said she couldn't believe that the inmates would strike because of taking their earrings and other personal items from them. I insisted that the captain allow me to lock up the ringleaders of the dorm but she said no.

In all of my experience working in prisons I learned to take heed to warnings. I knew if I locked up the ringleaders in the dorm, the other inmates wouldn't go forward with the food strike, because they didn't have a leader.

My cry fell on deaf ears, and this food strike would eventually bite the captain in the ass. Midday (lunch) the inmates did not report to eat at the dining hall. Out of thirteen hundred inmates maybe ten went to eat.

When I got to work Monday evening the inmates didn't report to the dining hall to eat. This was the first day of the food strike, and the administration had to do something. Tuesday morning the inmates didn't report to the dining hall to eat breakfast. Tuesday afternoon, the inmates didn't report to the dining hall to eat lunch and when I came to work at 4:00 p.m. the inmates *still* didn't go to the dining hall to eat dinner.

Even though the inmates were not reporting to the dining hall to eat, the food service department still had to cook for thirteen hundred people. This is the way it goes. So the food service department was cooking mounds of food and having to throw it out because no one was coming to eat. This cost the government money, time, and unnecessary energies.

I could see the administration panic and I could see the egg on the captain's face when she looked at me. I informed her if she'd let me lock up the ringleaders, this food strike would not have happened...prevention. The fact that she couldn't accept advice from a black lieutenant, because she thought black lieutenants were dumb, she had a serious strike on her hands.

I felt like this captain had a *serious* lack of knowledge about the responsibilities of a captain. She should never have been the captain of a prison. Two days went by and the food strike continued. Now the captain came to me and wanted to know who the ringleaders were because she wanted to lock them up. She hated asking me this question. I told her to go and ask the white special investigative lieutenant who the ringleaders were.

The inmates wouldn't give the white lieutenants any information. Most of the information the white lieutenants received was false. The captain and the warden panicked.

This food strike had gotten out of hand and the institution was in chaos. The captain gave instructions to start snatching anybody on the compound and take them to the bus in handcuffs and shackles.

This was the worst thing she could have ever done, because a lot of innocent inmates were put on buses to be transferred far away from home, because they were in the wrong place at the wrong time. I felt sorry for some of the inmates because I knew they were innocent.

It was raining hard and some of the inmates were crying, because they were put on buses and being transferred away from home; they knew it was going to be a long time before they were able to see their family members again. The inmates were being transferred to Miami.

Another mistake that the warden made, due to listening to the captain, was to suspend the family day visits for the inmates, because of the food strike. Family day was supposed to take place that Saturday.

Families had already started coming in from out of town and other countries to see their loved ones, but they didn't know were some of their loved ones were located, because they had been transferred. The institution made the decision to suspend the family day activities at the last minute; the inmates couldn't tell their loved ones not to come and visit that day.

Family day is a big event at the institution and is held once a year. It's like a big picnic for the inmates and their loved ones. This event usually takes place on the recreation field instead of the dining hall, because everyone on the inmate's visiting list is allowed to come in and visit.

Due to the fact that Captain Sullivan would not listen to me once again, a lot of unnecessary chaos, cost to the government, temporary displaced family members, inmates on the verge of losing their minds, and a lot of pressure on another facility (FDC Miami) that had to house these inmates in a section where they normally house others.

My career began with D.C. Department of Correction in 1987 and if you worked at that institution staff members would look or treat you as though you were corrupt. The Federal Bureau of Prisons always looked down on the staff that worked at Lorton (state prison in D.C. Department of Corrections at Lorton, Virginia), because they felt their system was better than Lorton. The real reason why they felt this way is because Lorton was run by an all black administration; Mayor Marion Berry from Washington, D.C. was in charge of the D.C. Department of Corrections (Lorton). What I came to realize after working with the Federal Bureau of Prisons, is that their system wasn't any better than Lorton. The Bureau of Prisons had dirty staff, and they had all kinds of illegal things going on just like Lorton. The staff in the Federal Bureau of Prisons wasn't any different than the staff at Lorton. Some staff was just crooked and you find that in any prison, not just at Lorton.

CHAPTER 31

Fair Sentencing Act of 2010

On November 04, 2008 when President Obama accepted the 44th President of the United States at Grant Park, Chicago Illinois, I can recall President Obama saying the first thing he wanted to do was reform the Criminal Justice System. President Obama made good on his promise when he signed into law "The Fair Sentencing Act of 2010." The Fair Sentencing Act of 2010 was an Act of Congress that was signed into Federal Law by U.S. President Barack Obama on August 03, 2010 that reduced the disparity between the amount of crack cocaine and powder cocaine needed to trigger certain federal criminal penalties from a 100:1 weight ratio.

The Fair Sentencing Act of 2010 reduced the disparity to 18 to 1. An offender would have to be convicted of peddling 28 grams or more of crack to be hit with a five year mandatory sentence. A 10 year prison term would be handed down for 280 grams or more. (Penalties for powder offenses are unchanged.) The legislation also eliminates a mandatory minimum sentence for simple possession.

With President Obama leading the way the United States Sentencing Commission is doing a lot to improve their sentence reductions. On July 18, 2014 the United States Sentencing Commission granted Full Retroactivity, their decision allowed federal drug prisoners to petition for sentence reductions. What does that mean?

It meant 46,290 federal drug prisoners can petition for sentence reductions. This was the largest number of Federal prisoners ever to benefit from a guideline amendment being made retroactive. Members of the Commission voted to make the amendment retroactive with no exclusions, though they did move the earliest possible release date from November 01, 2014, to November 2015.

When the Commission lowers sentences for future offenders, it has the option to make the reductions retroactive. Retroactivity allows prisoners to petition the federal courts for sentence reductions to match the sentences of incoming prisoners.

The Commission voted to make lower crack cocaine sentences retroactive for more than 24,000 prisoners in 2007 and 2011.

Allow me to give you an example of what I just said in layman terms. The Marshall Projects breaks it down like this. Let's say John Doe is one of the prisoners to be released later this month.

Doe was convicted of a federal drug crime several years ago. At the time, the federal judge who sentenced him probably consulted something called the Drug Quantity Table, which showed what "offense level" Doe deserved based on the type and amount of drug involved in his crime. The judge then used a separate table, called the Sentencing Table, to figure out how many years Doe would go to prison based on his offense level.

But the Sentencing Commission's new guidelines essentially instructed the courts to adjust Doe's offense level downward by two levels, which in turn meant that his sentence could be reduced, too. For instance, if Doe trafficked 80 to <100 grams of heroin, he used to be a Level 24 offender, and he was sentenced to prison for 51 to 63 months. When the guidelines changed, he was adjusted downward two levels to a Level 22 offender, and he was now eligible for a new sentence of 41 to 51 months.

Later on after my career with the Federal Bureau of Prison ended I would meet and work with Eric Sterling former counsel to the U.S. House Committee on the Judiciary, 1979-1989 and participate in the passage of the mandatory minimum sentencing laws. Currently, he is the President of The Criminal Justice Policy Foundation, Washington, D.C. and Co-Chair of the American Bar Association.

Mr. Sterling and I would eventually speak together in certain venues to bring attention to bias mandatory minimum sentences for drug offenses. Mr. Sterling stated, "The work that he was involved in in enacting the mandatory sentences is probably the greatest tragedy of his professional life and he suspects that the chairman of the subcommittee feels that way to. Mr. Sterling also stated, "There have been literally thousands of instances of injustice where minor co-conspirators in cases, the lowest level participants, have been given the sentences that Congress intended for the highest kingpins. Families are wrecked, children are orphaned, and taxpayers are paying a fortune for excessive punishment. You know there's nothing conservative about punishing people too much. That's an excess and it's just a waste. It is such a waste of human life. The war on drugs is one of the great evils of our times."

CHAPTER 32

How It All Began

The beginning of mass incarceration started in 1971 when President Nixon waged a war on drugs when his administration created the mandatory sentencing laws drugs laws (Rockefellers). In 1986 when professional ball player Lin Bias died of cocaine overdose and when the use of crack cocaine became prevalent Congress caved in to the public pressure to be harder on crime.

This was also an election year and the Speaker of the House Tip O'Neill and the democrats pushed their agenda to be harder on crime and the public brought it, hook, line and sinker and the 1986 Anti-Drug Abuse Act was born and signed into law by President Regan on October 27, 1986. He continued President Nixon's legacy and doubled down on the war on drugs. Crack cocaine was considered an African American problem and powder cocaine was a White American problem. The two drugs were the same but the sentencing guidelines were different, this was evident when the court system meted out longer prison sentences to African Americans and Latinos than whites when they were arrested for illegally possessing powder and crack cocaine.

In 1971 the prison population was 200,000 when the war on drugs started and in the 90's under President Clinton the prison population shot up to 2.5 million Our prison population grew over 900 percent and today we incarcerate more people than any other country in the world. After the crack era ended we continued our war on drugs and in 2014 there were more than 1.5 million drugs arrests more than 80 percent of the arrests were for possession only and half of that was for marijuana which in some states is legal.

In essence we are spending 80 billion dollars a year to incarcerate in this country for the war on drugs including marijuana and now the United States is making 50 billion a year off the sale of legal marijuana. It's ironic that same people who were incarcerated for possession and selling marijuana while it was illegal cannot go to another state where marijuana is legal and open up a marijuana dispensary shop to sell legal marijuana.

The rate of drug use is as high as it were 50 years ago when President Nixon declared the war on drugs. The country has awakened and realized a lot of people were incarcerated because of an addiction and now they are considering this a health problem. It saddens me to know that drug treatment centers were phased out when minorities were struggling with their addiction of crack cocaine and so therefore they were sent to prison for long periods of time. Now that the drug methamphetamine is on the rise and not a drug of choice by minorities the government is building drug treatment centers to ensure non minorities don't go to prison.

CHAPTER 33

A New Presidency Voted In

The American people have spoken and they elected Donald Trump to be the 45th President of the United States of America. Although the polls had secretary of State Hillary Clinton winning prior and the day of the election, something went wrong. I'm 56 years old and the 2016 Presidential election exposed an America of deep divides over, culture, ethnicity and race! I've never seen a campaign so divisive and what I'm seeing in America is something I never thought I would see and that is we are on a brink of a civil war.

On November 08, 2016 I used my constitutional rights to vote for Hillary Clinton. I usually vote for candidates that catered to the issues that I'm concerned about and that is criminal justice reform. Over the last 18 months I never heard Donald Trump address or said anything about criminal justice reform.

I wanted poetic justice for Hillary Clinton in a sense that she could continue the criminal justice reform that President

Barack Obama has started. If Hillary would have been elected she could have corrected the mass incarceration problem that her husband President Clinton caused when he signed The Violent Crime Control Law Enforcement Act that triple the mass incarceration.

I voted for Hillary Clinton because just in case you didn't know, today in America, more than one out of every 100 adults is behind bars. This mass incarceration epidemic has an explicit racial bias, as one in three black men can expect to go to prison in their lifetime. A significant number of those incarcerated are held for low-level, nonviolent offenses. On former Secretary of State Hilliary Clinton she suggested from her website We must end the era of mass incarceration by:

A. Reforming mandatory minimum sentencing. Excessive federal mandatory minimum sentences keep nonviolent drug offenders in prison for too long—and have increased racial inequality in our criminal justice system. Hillary wanted to reform this system by:

- Cutting mandatory minimum sentences for nonviolent drug offenses in half.
- Allowing current nonviolent prisoners to seek fairer sentences.
- Eliminating the sentencing disparity for crack and powder cocaine so that equal amounts of crack and powder cocaine carry equal sentences, and applying this change retroactively.
- Reforming the "strike" system, so that nonviolent drug offenses no longer count as a "strike," reducing

the mandatory penalty for second- and third-strike offenses.

Focusing federal enforcement resources on violent crime, not simple marijuana pos-session. Marijuana arrests, including for simple possession, account for a large number of drug arrests. Significant racial disparities exist in marijuana enforcement—black men are significantly more likely to be arrested for marijuana possession than their white counter-parts, despite the fact that their usage rates are similar. Hillary wanted to allow states that have enacted marijuana laws to act as laboratories of democracy and reschedule marijuana from a Schedule I to a Schedule II substance.

Prioritizing treatment and rehabilitation—rather than incarceration—for low-level, nonviolent drug offenders. More than half of prison and jail inmates suffer from a mental health problem. Up to 65 percent of the correctional population meets the medical criteria for a substance use disorder. Hillary wanted to ensure law enforcement is properly trained for crisis intervention and referral to treatment as appropriate, directing the attorney general to urge federal prosecutors to seek treatment over incarceration for low-level, nonviolent drug crimes.

Hillary wanted to dismantle the school-to-prison pipeline. She wanted to work to dismantle the school-to-prison pipeline by providing $2 billion in support to schools to reform overly punitive disciplinary policies, calling on states to reform school disturbance laws, and encouraging states to use federal education funding to implement social and emotional support interventions.

Ending the privatization of prisons. Hillary believes we should move away from contracting out this core responsibility of the federal government to private corporations. We must not create private industry incentives that may contribute—or have the appearance of contributing—to over-incarceration. The campaign does not accept contributions from federally registered lobbyists or PACs for private prison companies and will donate any such direct contributions to charity.

Promote successful re-entry by formerly incarcerated individuals.

In 2016, the number of people released from state or federal prison will reach approximately 600,000. For the sake of everyone given a second chance—as well as the health and safety of the communities to which they return—the pathway to re-entry should offer a fair opportunity for success. Hillary wanted to work to remove barriers and create pathways to employment, housing, health care, education, and civic participation, including:

- Taking executive action to "ban the box" for federal employers and contractors, so that applicants have an opportunity to demonstrate their qualifications before being asked about their criminal records.
- Investing $5 billion in re-entry job programs for formerly incarcerated individuals so that individuals can have a fair shot at getting back on their feet and becoming productive, contributing members of society.
- Supporting legislation to restore voting rights to individuals who have served their sentences.

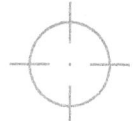

EPILOGUE

While I was in my mother's womb God had already commissioned me to make a change. I was born on January 25, 1964. During the year of my birth, the world decided it needed to create the Civil Rights Act of 1964. When Barack Obama started preaching change, I had already started making a difference with my fight for civil rights. I am a leader that does not hold back on the truth and that is why I have caught so much hell and continue to catch hell for telling you the raw truth.

When slavery began that's when black families were separated. God destined man to be the head of the household, but when women saw their husbands taken away and treated less than human it created a vicious cycle that is still going on today. Most women don't have a man in the house to help raise their children because most black men are under some form of supervision under the criminal justice system.

In addition to this black women in prison are on the rise leaving the black children to raise themselves. These facts will contribute to the black race becoming extinct. We (blacks) used to be the *second* largest population in the United States, but now we are *third* largest population in the United States.

Studies show more than one in every one hundred adults in America is in jail or prison, as is one in nine black men between the ages of twenty and thirty-four, according to a new report. That's more than any other nation. Fifty states spent more than 80 billion dollars on corrections. More money is being spent to build prisons than on colleges. Last but not least, in today's society, a black male has a one-in-three chance of going to prison in his lifetime. This must change.

Congratulations to Barack Obama who was the first elected African American President of the United States on November 4, 2008…by the people for the people! Meet me in Washington D.C. for the Presidential Inauguration January 20, 2009!

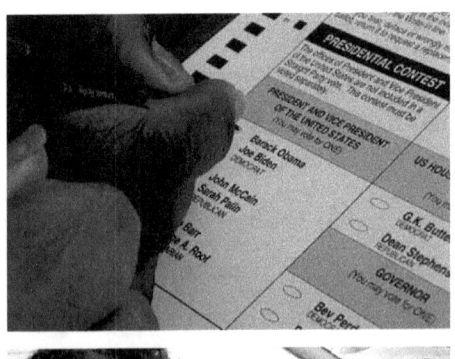

The top photo is the fingers of my Grandmother, Mrs. Tessie Jones and my Aunt Mavis Colleen Jones. They were at the early voting for the Presidential Campaign in Kinston, N.C. between Barack Obama and John Mccain.

The second photo is my grandmother returning the in*k* pen to the poll person after participating in the history-making voting process for the first Black President. A few days prior to this, my grandmother had just buried her youngest son Earl "Hamm" Jones. Fortunately, she was able to see President Barack Obama on television accepting the Presidency on November 04, 2008. She'd encouraged me to attend the Inauguration on January 20, 2009. While on my way to attend the Inauguration my grandmother passed (January 16, 2009).

-Garry Jones

www.garryjones.com

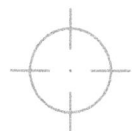

REFERENCES

1. United States Sentencing Commission, *Special Report to Congress: Cocaine and Federal Sentencing Policy*, 1995, Washington, D.C. 1995 p. 156.
2. Anti-Drug Abuse Act (1986) Major Acts of Congress, by Daryl K. Brown, www.enotes.com/ major-acts- congress/ anti-drug-abuse-act
3. Drug Laws and Snitching: A Primer by Eric E. Sterling, www.pbs.org/wgbh/pages/frontline/ shows/snitch/primer
4. ACLU Release Crack Cocaine Report Anti-Drug Abuse of 1986 Deepened Racial Inequity in Sentencing (10/26/2006), www.aclu.org/ drugpolicy/ gen/27194prs20061026.html
5. Parole…verbatim from the U.S. Department of Justice, www.momy.org/parole.htm
6. Our Documents – Civil Rights Act (1964), www.ourdocuments.gov/doc.php?doc=97
7. www.hillaryclinton.com
8. www.the marshallproject.org
9. https:www.ussc.gov/research/congressional-reports/2015-report-congress-impact-fair-sentencing-act-2010

www.ingramcontent.com/pod-product-compliance
Lightning Source LLC
Chambersburg PA
CBHW070606300426
44113CB00010B/1431